Bibliographie de la philosophie

au Canada: une guide à recherche

Bibliography of Philosophy in

Canada: a Research Guide

D1373931

FRYE LIBRARY OF CANADIAN PHILOSOPHY
General Editor: J. Douglas Rabb

The Library will include volumes on:
William Lyall
William Albert Crawford-Frost
Charles De Koninck
George Paxton Young
Jacob Gould Schurman
George John Blewett
Herbert Leslie Stewart
John Clark Murray
John Watson

Already published:
Religion and Science in Early Canada

Bibliographie de la philosophie

au Canada: une guide à recherche

Bibliography of Philosophy in

Canada: a Research Guide
Thomas Mathien

Version française
Louise Girard
&
Lori Morris

FRYE LIBRARY OF CANADIAN PHILOSOPHY
SUPPLEMENTARY VOLUME ONE

Ronald P. Frye & Company

ISBN 0 919741 74 6

Copyright © 1989 Ronald P. Frye & Company

Published by
Ronald P. Frye & Company
273 King Street East
Kingston, Ontario Canada K7L 3B1
Phone (613) 545-1308

All rights reserved. No part of this publication may be reproduced or transmitted in any form or by any means, electronic or mechanical, including photocopy, recording or information storage and retrieval system.

There are a number of people without whom this work, and the body of information whichlies behind it, would have been impossible. J.T. Stevenson's organizational efforts, as principal investigator for the Bibliography of Philosophy in Canada, along with his support and encouragement, were essential. John Slater and Roland Houde, true bibliophiles, taught me much and contributed much to the project. Myrna Friend taught me a lot about the techniques employed here and Margaret McGrath, one-time reference librarian at St. Michael's College, showed me ingenious ways to extend the search. I learned a great deal about the character of Canadian intellectual history from authors: Leslie Armour, Elizabeth Trott, Carl Berger, Ramsay Cook, Yvan Lamonde, and A.B. McKillop. They are all to be thanked. In addition, thanks are due to those who served as researchers for the project. Although I trained many of them, I learned a great deal more from their inventiveness. They are: Steve Anderson, Shelley Appleby, Katherine Arima, Michael Bedard, Emilio Bettiga, Martin Donougho, Blake Landor, Karen McIntosh, Steve Smith, Lyn Straka. Lori Morris, also one of their number, deserves special mention. Her association was longest, and her skills as both a linguist and an historian of letters were particularly valuable. She also shares the translation honors for this effort. It is to her and to Louise Girard that I owe whatever sense the French text makes. Finally, Shelagh Stevenson deserves mention for her skill, patience and powers of observation, all exercised in reducing the manuscript to a form presentable to the publisher.

Printed & Bound in Canada

UNIVERSITY LIBRARY
181591 Lethbridge, Alberta

Table of Contents

Introduction

Audience and Field

This guide is divided into three parts. The first part is a general guide to the techniques and instruments available to those who wish to do bibliographic research on publications by Canadians in philosophy and related areas. The second part is a list of important existing bibliographic and historical sources for information on philosophy done by Canadians. The third part details important published works by English Canadian philosophers active before 1950. The remarks which serve as an introduction will establish the utility of these parts and that of a general bibliography of philosophy in Canada. In addition a specification of the field of study will be suggested and defended.

Although philosophy is a discipline in which many practitioners have been content to master the literature in an area of interest informally, the success of the publications of the Philosophy Documentation Center and especially of the *Philosopher's Index* and the associated computer search service indicate that, as the philosophic community and its interest expand and become more complex, organized means of access to public discussions of philosophical issues become increasingly welcome. A general bibliography of Canadian work in philosophy is of use philosophers. It will also help intellectual historians.

All philosophers in Canada will find the bibliography a useful record of what their colleagues have done. Where the interest is only in contemporary work, such a bibliography will provide an extension of material already retrievable through the *Philosopher's Index* and the *Répertoire bibliographique de philosophie*, organized, perhaps, in an order more useful for some purposes: by author for example, rather than by year and then by author. Philosophers who consider historical issues may find in such a bibliography information on earlier Canadian thinkers not readily available in any source. This guide will provide the means for assembling references to works by and about thinkers not indexed in the standard sources for current bibliography. Many of the techniques presented, and some of the instruments listed, can also be generalized to provide guidance for other bio-bibliographic projects in philosophy and related fields.

Some philosophers think that it is important to reflect on the philosophic traditions existing within the cultures of English Canada and Quebec. Such historical reflection might, shed light on the nature of philosophy and indicate whether the Canadian cultures have generated anything important to be placed on the philosophic agenda. There are several distinct reasons to think so. One is the idealistic belief that various cultures express and live out the consequences of ideas and theories which are somehow appropriate to them and that philosophy represents an important part of the culture's reflections on its mental life. A second very different justification lies in the Marxist view that a philosophy or group of philosophies in a society reflects, and to some lesser extent reacts on, the social conflicts in the society. To understand their genuine import, it will be necessary, first, to get an idea of the sort of philosophical doctrines current in the society and their relative importance and, second, make the connection between them and the conflicts with which they are associated.

Thinkers of historicist or relativistic bent will also find a general bibliography useful. They can use it to gain an understanding of the special character of a nation's philosophic contribution. If they are not members of the group with which they are concerned their motives may be essentially ethnological. If they are, they may crave self-understanding. The historicist may wish to fit the results into a broader picture; the relativist will think that impossible. Whatever their concerns, they will have to determine what philosophic works a society has produced before they can characterize its "national" philosophy. Even those who doubt that it is possible to describe a national philosophy--or group of national philosophies in a multi-national state--may find in the resources presented in this guide, or in the bibliography generated from it, means to support their position or to defeat those who attempt such descriptions.

As mentioned, philosophers are, by no means, the only group with an interest in a record of Canadian philosophical writings. Intellectual historians will benefit from access to some of the most abstract and general ideological productions of the country. These writings might not have had a great deal of influence on daily life at the time of production, but may very well provide an interesting reflection of the general frame of mind and the underlying assumptions, of at least the intellectual classes at the time of their production. They can do this because of their abstractness and generality. Since they are removed from the specifics of the political and economic debates of their time, they will not be as colored by narrow party considerations as would the journalistic, the economic, the political, or even the historical writings of the period. Differences among the producers of philosophical pieces, especially differences worth being called differences of intellectual style and movement, could indicate deep differences in the society at large.

The sort of information to which this guide can provide access will help decide historical issues. Were nineteenth- century Canadian intellectuals, perhaps in contrast with their American counterparts, primarily religious and moralistic rather than skeptical and critical?[1] Do various individuals exhibit different levels of skepticism or moralism? What explanation might be offered for these differences or for the pattern they exhibit? Good bio-bibliographic tools will make it easier to develop the broad acquaintance with the philosophic literature of the period required to answer these questions.

With these tools, more complete surveys can be made of the published views of Canadian thinkers on such matters as the importance of science, or their beliefs about human nature and the foundations of morality. One can also discover how the views of various writers on these matters differed with their social and ethnic origins, their social positions, and those of their intended audience. This will permit the testing of various hypotheses about the intellectual history of the country.

In addition there are a number of producers of philosophy in Canada who interest the historians as more than mere reflections of socially important attitudes. Among them, the cultivated amateurs and the influential professionals are particularly noteworthy. The former are not principally engaged in writing and teaching in philosophy but do deal with such topics from time to time, as a part of their intellectual activities. Some examples are William Dawson LeSueur and Goldwin Smith in English Canada and Etienne Parent in Quebec. The influential professionals are those philosophers whose published work or teaching has helped to form the views of people active in other fields. John Watson, whose views influenced the founders of the United Church, is one. So are George Parkin Grant[2], Charles DeKoninck, Louis-Adolphe Pâquet, and Cardinal Villeneuve. Moreover, there are important philosophers whose work in that field is but one part of a many-faceted career. One might mention Emil Fackenheim and Francis Sparshott, François Hertel, and Jean Le Moyne. There are also academics who hold chairs and have influence in fields other than philosophy, but who have made important philosophic contributions. Among these, for example, are C.B. Macpherson, John O'Neill, and Fernand Dumont.

In some cases, debates which have philosophical overtones have accompanied important historical developments. This is certainly so in Quebec where the rise of--and opposition to--the Institut canadien, the impact of the thought of De Lammenais, the development of ultramontanism, and disputes over political liberalism have all had both philosophical and socio-political aspects. This connection is less obvious in English Canada, but even there, the link of certain strains of idealism with imperialism and of other strains with the rise of the United Church and with the social gospel movement has been noted.[3] Richard Maurice Bucke led efforts to reform the treatment of those judged insane. His actions were based on peculiar views on the relation of moral dispositions to traits of the nervous system and on views about the adaptive advantages which certain of these dispositions afforded to those who had them.

Nevertheless, the social historian will be more interested in philosophic doctrines as reflections and effects of social conditions than as important influences on them. The views of philosophers have a broad impact only when large numbers of people accept them and can apply them. This usually does not happen until after they have been filtered through a large number of intermediaries.[4]

What sort of writings should the bibliographer count as sufficiently philosophical to report in a bibliography, to provide means to locate in a guide? No academic discipline has clear boundaries separating its area of concern from those of others. The frontiers become even more fuzzy when the discipline is viewed diachronically. The principle most appropriate to general, historical bibliographies would seem to be that of maximum justifiable inclusiveness.

Bibliographic tools providing access to Canadian philosophy must serve social historians with various, and perhaps also vague, notions of philosophy. Many of them will be primarily interested in the links between whatever they take the discipline to be and other fields. In addition, the boundaries of the discipline have shifted. Even those who want to reserve the term 'philosophy' for subjects usually taught by academic departments of philosophy admit this fact. Moreover, philosophers and students of philosophy have widely different views about what philosophy is. Since the production of a general institutional bibliography of philosophy or of tools to assist locations of items in that field must serve all philosophers, and aid historians interested in a number of periods of intellectual history, the urge to restrict the range of references should be resisted.

For this reason references to a large number of writings in the now independent field of psychology must be included. Psychology was taught as a branch of philosophy through the early part of the century at the University of Toronto. It was taught along with philosophy at Dalhousie and at the University of British Columbia until much later. The faculties of philosophy at Université d'Ottawa and Université de Montréal included departments of psychology until well past mid-century. Until the mid 1960's, an introductory psychology course was listed as part of the philosophy program at St. Michael's College in the University of Toronto. Although it continued to be listed for some years after it had ceased to be given, it remained on the books as long as it did because many philosophers in the Catholic tradition believed that psychology and other human sciences ought to be philosophically informed. The guide, therefore, indicates some tools useful for locating the published contributions of these early psychologists.

Some tools can also be used to locate writings which might be classed as social scientific. Many of the earliest social scientists, such as Adam Smith, John Stuart Mill, Max Weber and Emile Durkheim, were also trained as philosophers. Nineteenth and early twentieth-century philosophy in English Canada still bore a close relation to social scientific endeavors. Some major contemporary figures in the social sciences have been recruited from philosophy.[5] In Quebec, the development of autonomous departments in many of the social sciences has occurred only since World War II. At Queen's, a university in the Scottish tradition during the nineteenth century, subjects such as political economy were frequently assigned to those who held the chair of philosophy.[6] Even now, the work of scholars in fields closely tied to social scientific research, such as game theory and decision theory, has an influence on philosophy in English Canada. Consequently, some works which could be regarded as works of general social scientific theory have a place in a general bibliography of philosophy in Canada.

Clearly then, works from fields no longer counted as part of philosophy must be noted especially when philosophers, present or past, regard them as crucial to their own philosophic studies. No judgement of the quality of the work should affect the decision to include. Just as the archaeologist includes in a survey of the ceramic industry of a culture both fine and badly-made pieces, so the general bibliographer catalogues the bad bits as well as the intellectual masterpieces.

Such a policy will produce a very large list of references. Organized according to author, there is probably adequate guidance for a researcher interested in a particular individual. Provision of additional routes of access will also help the searcher. If each item is assigned a cluster of subject categories and means are provided to trace items by date and language as well, then the task of locating information will be greatly simplified. The bibliography generated by the techniques and tools provided in this guide will be designed to permit searching by these categories. In addition, the tools and techniques presented here will aid in the compilation of more specialized bibliographies, a number of which are included in Part II.

A general bibliography of philosophy in Canada will, therefore, have a great number of references to works which are hard to classify as clear examples of philosophy but which are at least equally hard to classify as belonging to any other discipline.[7] It will contain items with rather little philosophic content but which, nevertheless, are examples of what immediately precedes and sets the ideological stage for philosophic writing.[8] Also to be included are the works of non- philosophers which have had impact either directly on philosophers or on the intellectual environment which has helped to form them. Consequently, some works by the theorists of communication, Harold Innis and Marshall McLuhan, are to be listed. Studies of historical figures who are of interest to workers in more than one discipline should be recorded. Thus, discussions of theological interest on Augustine, Aquinas, or Bonaventure; literary studies of Nietzsche, theological studies of Kierkegaard, and treatments of the "philosophical" aspects of the work of Newton, Darwin, Einstein or Durkheim must be included. The work of people in closely related disciplines such as that of the classicist G.M.A. Grube belongs in our bibliography. Finally, non-philosophic works by practicing Canadian philosophers should be included to indicate how philosophy has influenced other fields. For this reason the studies on Social Credit in Alberta done by John Irving and C.B. Macpherson should be included.

There are three possible rules for deciding whether work which counts as "philosophical" is also "Canadian." The first rule regards those interested in philosophy in a particular country during a certain period as a community which both produces and consumes philosophic writings. This community's level of development during a given year could be measured by a record of the writings it produced and consumed during the year. However, a bibliography replete with works written and published in Scotland or France or the United States (or Germany or ancient Greece) by citizens of those countries would not be useful to the researcher with standard expectations about the contents of a bibliography of Canadian philosophers--although a record of what was read or commented on by students and practitioners in philosophy, or records of the contents of such people's libraries, would have an important place in a *history* of the discipline and its community.

A case could be made for the inclusion of all things written by Canadians and all things published in Canada. Some bibliographies, notably Landry's record of Canadian contributions on medieval philosophy, follow this practice.[9] It could be suggested that listing the philosophical product of Canadian publishing institutions will assist in developing a picture of the philosophic community because it will help scholars to determine the significance and international impact of the community (it could be suggested that a community is very important when it includes publishing institutions which issue a wide variety of works by contributors from elsewhere), and to give at least some indication of what is produced for domestic consumption.

This first inclusion policy has shortcomings, however. Some books published in Canada are issued by Canadian subsidiaries of international publishers for the Canadian market because of convenience or copyright reasons. In other cases, rights agreements will be made between local publishers and foreign firms under which an edition of an internationally significant book, differing, perhaps, only in the title page from that of its principal publisher, will be issued by the Canadian firm for the local market.

Some journal articles are also misleading. Although the existence of specialized journals such as *Mediaeval Studies* provides an important indication of fairly high levels of academic development in Canada, they are, nevertheless, aimed at a largely non-Canadian audience. An item in such a journal produced by a German for an audience scattered over Europe and the Americas will not be truly representative of Canadian philosophic activity, even if it should number some Canadians among its readers. In addition, there are journals which exist largely as academic pastimes of their editors. If such a person gets an academic position in Canada, then the journal may also migrate for the duration of the appointment, however brief. *Telos* is associated with Paul Piccone. He spent some time in the Sociology Department at the University of Toronto. This should not be sufficient to Canadianize the journal or its non-Canadian contributors.

Nowadays, Canadian journals perform another function which causes problems for this first rule. There is a great deal of pressure on academics to publish. In philosophy, the major journals in English-speaking North America have rejection rates as high as 90 per cent. This means that many authors are circulating manuscripts all over the English-speaking world, sending them to journals which may not be second rate, but may be in the second rank as far as professional influence is concerned. Even journals which have readerships located mainly in particular countries or regions will be recipients of these manuscripts. Canadian journals seem to fall into this category and become, thereby, outlets for the work of philosophers from other countries.

While Canadian (and other) journals have recently provided mastheads of convenience for writings produced elsewhere, quite another bibliographically misleading thing occurred in the more distant past. The nineteenth-century intellectual journal was hungry for readable copy aimed at an audience both of non-specialists and of specialists in various fields. In some areas, and English-speaking Canada was one of them; demand for copy sometimes outran supply. One option open to the editors of such journals was to solicit or simply reprint pieces produced elsewhere. This option was especially attractive when the pieces were first published in places with a reputation of cultural superiority. Many articles printed in the *Canadian Monthly and National Review* were from British sources. Some, such as those by George John Romanes, were produced by former Canadians who had established a good reputation in Britain.[10] Others were simply products of authors who wrote on matters judged by editors to be of interest to educated Canadians. These types of foreign contribution indicate that the local intellectual community is not entirely capable of self-sufficiency, that it is still in a colonial state. In this case, as in the others, the presence of such writings is important and ought to be noted in histories, but their listing in a general bibliography could be misleading.

The second approach to documenting the discipline would include only references to the products of Canadian authors. The bibliographer then becomes a literary archaeologist cataloguing all the accessible products and all evidences of the tools of a certain kind of intellectual industry. This is a much more restrictive approach than the first, because it leaves out many bibliographically misleading records. It also excludes some valuable items, such as the imported text books which had such a great influence on the views both of philosophers and the educated general public, e.g., the *Institutiones* used in Quebec and in Catholic colleges in English Canada, and the works of Paley, Bain, and McCosh used in the rest of English Canada. No reference would be made to any imported works which may have had a great impact and generated a great deal of discussion but occasioned no published comments. Works of very influential expatriates who had no extensive professional career in Canada would be omitted regardless of their influence on Canadians. A general bibliography is an aid to the historian, but it need not solve all reference problems of historians nor replace their descriptive efforts.

Such a catalogue of intellectual artifacts provides no means to judge the relative importance of the items to which it refers. One would like to know how much these products were used both at home and abroad. One would like to know if the Canadian producers of philosophical ideas were, in fact, a community with a great deal of mutual contact or a group of isolated brain workers, each with a local audience but cut off from each other. The bibliographer can provide some information about overall importance of a work by reporting new printings, new editions and translations of a work, wherever they are traceable. Geographical extent of an author's influence can be indicated in a partial way simply by reporting the existence of items which have been published outside Canada. Some insight into the nature of the intellectual community into which the author fits can be gained from records of published comments on the author's work.

The third inclusion policy admits all such items into it and associates with each author the appropriate commentaries. This is the policy which was followed by researchers for the Bibliography of Philosophy in Canada, who also filed material by Canadians about Canadians with both the author and the subject philosopher in order to permit some determination of the extent to which there is a network of Canadian philosophers.

The limitations of this policy must be acknowledged. It is difficult to provide a complete list of translations, reprints, new editions, and commentaries. Items about Canadian authors can only be traced through existing indexes, the subject catalogues of libraries, and certain standard but restricted Canadian bibliographical sources. Translations into non-European languages are difficult to trace, especially if they were made a long time ago. It is not generally possible to record all the reprints of frequently reprinted books, nor will there be any indication of the extent of each print run. New editions, especially new editions of translations, are frequently hard to trace.

Exactly what will be found for each author will vary as a result of a complex of factors, some systematic (When did the author work? What periods do the indexes cover?) and some purely individual (Who provided the subject categorization in the *Philosopher's Index* for articles published by a particular journal in a particular year?). It is not even possible, therefore, to suggest that the items reported in the bibliographic sources represent a uniform percentage of the items in this category. Thus, the most that can be gained from a bibliography organized like the B.P.C. are suggestions rather than clear indications of an author's importance. These suggestions do, however, indicate a lower limit of the influence of each author, and they may well prove quite useful to the intellectual historian. The contents of the commentaries and revisions mentioned may advance the understanding of the historian of philosophy.

Part I

Guide to Research on the History of Philosophy in Canada

There are two problems faced by people who want to compile bibliographies for authors of some category. First, they must compose and verify a list of authors in the category writing on the topics to which the bibliography is dedicated. Then they must compile and verify a list of works produced by these authors in the specified fields. The techniques and instruments discussed in this section will permit the solution of these problems for Canadians working in philosophy and closely related fields.[11]

How can one find out which Canadians have done work in philosophy? In recent years the philosopher has almost always had the university as a habitat. More often than not, the philosopher can be found in university departments of philosophy and on the membership lists of philosophical associations. University calendars and the membership lists of the Canadian Philosophical Association for particular years indicate who was active during those years. This information may be difficult to obtain at any single location, but there are shortcuts for certain periods. The *Directory of American Philosophers* also lists Canadian philosophers teaching at reporting institutions. Annual volumes can be consulted both for information about individuals recently active in the field and for data on the size and composition of philosophy departments. The *Directory*'s listing of graduate assistants as well as fulltime teachers is useful but can mislead.[12]

Another useful source is the *Directory of American Scholars*. It contains biographies for many Canadian philosophers (and other scholars in the humanities), and each four-volume edition has a general index. It has appeared in a number of editions, the most recent of which takes the directory to 1985. It lists only active academics and those who have recently left the field, so back issues need to be checked for people who have died or retired. While no edition is complete even for people active at the time of issuance, its biographical sketches do provide detail about professional history and academic interests and help in cases where there is some doubt about nationality or fields of endeavor. Faculty lists for universities in the British Commonwealth can be found in the *Commonwealth Universities Yearbook*. This source can be very useful for periods predating the availability of other directories. The annual membership lists of the Canadian Philosophical Association report members of philosophy departments and also many people professionally active in philosophy, but lacking teaching appointments in that field.

Other reliable sources for names include histories of religious orders, histories of the various universities and colleges, university presidents' reports, university archival materials, and histories of philosophy departments and related university departments. A selection of such sources is included in Part II. When dealing with histories of departments and records in sources such as the *Commonwealth Universities Yearbook*, care must be taken to note the existence of multi-department faculties of philosophy. As mentioned, such faculties existed at the Université de Montréal and the Université d'Ottawa until recently. These faculties may include departments of psychology, medieval studies, and education. A reference to a teacher in the faculty of philosophy in such an institution should be checked to determine whether the individual taught philosophy or some other, related subject. Similarly, early departments of philosophy in several universities, notably the University of Toronto, included psychologists among their number. Special care must be taken to determine whether members of such departments fall in, or fall between, contemporary classifications.[13]

One additional and very valuable source of information on philosophers is Karl Klinck's *Literary History of Canada*. Both the first edition and the updated three-volume edition contain chapters on philosophic writing in English Canada. In addition, there are chapters on essay writing and writing in theology, the social sciences, and the natural sciences which provide leads on writers whose work overlaps disciplinary boundaries.

There are many means to confirm the identity of people listed as philosophers. When the death date of a nineteenth-century author has been established, then the existing volumes of the *Dictionary of Canadian Biography* can be searched for biographical details. People whose deaths do not fall into the periods already covered by the published volumes of this source can be checked in William Stewart Wallace's *Macmillan Dictionary of Canadian Biography*. Also useful are the *Canadian Who's Who* and Henry J. Morgan's *Canadian Men and Women of the Time* (1898 and 1912). The nationality of more recent philosophers can sometimes be determined from the *International Directory of Philosophy and Philosophers*, a comprehensive list of philosophers and philosophical institutions outside North America (the most recent edition is 1986-89, published in 1986). Biographies of natural and social scientists whom one suspects of active interest in philosophical matters can be had from the various editions of *American Men and Women of Science* and its predecessor *American Men of Science*. Brief biographies of important Quebec authors can be found, along with short bibliographies in the *Dictionnaire pratique des auteurs québécois* by Reginald Hamel, John Hare, and Paul Wyczynski (1976).

Cases where nationality or period of activity in Canada remain in doubt can sometimes be dealt with by consulting biographical sources from other countries. Noteworthy British sources include the *Academic Who's Who, Who was Who, Who's Who,* and the *Dictionary of National Biography*. These can also be useful in tracing notable Canadians who expatriated themselves for lengthy periods. *Who's Who in America* and the American *Who was Who* are useful as are such directories of American biography as the *National Cyclopaedia of American Biography* and the *Dictionary of American Biography*. Also helpful are the various regional and specialized versions of *Who's Who*. In addition, French, Spanish, Dutch, and German versions of *Who's Who* can be consulted, as well as historical guides to French literature.

In Quebec and in many of the Catholic institutions in English Canada, many of the writers on philosophic topics have been clerics. Biographical information on such people can be found in a number of special sources. Various editions of *Canada ecclésiastique* may be checked for locations of priests at the time each was compiled. French Canadian priests active before 1936 are likely to have biographies in Jean-Baptiste-Arthur Allaire's *Dictionnaire biographique du clergé canadien-français* (1910+; 6 vols.) Deceased Canadian Oblates of Mary Immaculate have biographies in the three volumes of Gaston Carrière's *Dictionnaire biographique des Oblats de Marie-Immaculée au Canada* (1976) and deceased Basilians are recorded in Robert Scollard's *Dictionary of Basilian Biography*.

Once the philosophers are found, one must find their works. The techniques required vary according to the period in which the philosophers were active. It is easy to construct extensive, though not exhaustive, lists of works by people active in recent years. The two principal instruments are the *Philosopher's Index* produced by the Philosophy Documentation Center in Bowling Green, Ohio, and the *Répertoire bibliographique de la philosophie,* produced at Louvain. The former was first issued in 1967 and currently includes an author index with abstracts for many of the articles, an extensive subject index, a book review index, and lists of translations. It indexes journals in several languages, but is best for English-language publications. It is accompanied by two sets of retrospective volumes covering the period 1940-1966 for journals and 1940-1976 for books. The first set documents English- language publications from the United States, while the second indexes English-language publications from outside the United States. Each contains an author index with some abstracts and an extensive subject index. Book reviews are included only when they are major review articles. The *Philosopher's_Index* is a very good tool for locating items by subject and a good but limited means for finding items by author.

The *Répertoire bibliographique de la philosophie* does not permit such extensive and precise searches by subject, but its author list is less limited. Begun in 1949, it is a successor to the bibliographic issues of the *Revue philosophique de Louvain* and those of the *Tijdschrift voor filosofie* with which it shares its organizing principles. It attempts to provide a comprehensive index for philosophical publications in English, French, German, Italian, Spanish, Portuguese, Dutch, and Catalan. It also provides some coverage of items written in other European languages. It indexes scholarly articles, pamphlets, monographs, and the contents of some collections of articles and Festschriften. Entries are grouped according to broad subject categories, and a name index is provided at the end of each year's final volume. This index provides access to articles about, as well as by the people listed. The final issue also provides a list of book reviews indexed during the year, organized alphabetically according to the authors of the books reviewed or according to titles when they lack true authors. The *Répertoire* is the single most useful tool for anyone compiling a bibliography of post World War II philosophical work in any field, excluding technical studies in mathematical logic. It is especially valuable because it lists pre-1967 publications in a wide variety of languages, in addition to the contents of many collections. Items in collections, whether newly published or reprinted whether found in anthologies, Festschriften, or publications of conference proceedings, are among the most difficult items to retrieve. The *Répertoire* may also be used to collect book reviews by an author. The method for doing so, however, is tricky and time-consuming. One should read the instructions to the user carefully before beginning this kind of search.

Additional articles in collections can sometimes be discovered through the *Bibliographie de la philosophie* which, since 1954, has listed monographs together with abstracts of their contents. These abstracts, together with each volume's index(es) of authors, contributors, translators, and editors mentioned in the abstracts, can provide clues to the existence of individual contributors not marked elsewhere. Other contributions to collections of philosophical writings can sometimes be located through the *Essay and General Literature Index* (1900+), through the *Canadian Book Review Annual* (1975+), and rarely, in the short-lived *Canadian Essays and Collections Index 1971-2*.

The *Répertoire* and its predecessor may be supplemented by G.A. DeBrie's *Bibliographia Philosophica*, published at Louvain, which is organized in a manner similar to that of the *Répertoire* and covers the period 1934 to 1945. The period between the mid 1930's and 1949 is also covered by the *Répertoire's* predecessor and by the *Bibliographie de la philosophie* which was a general but not very comprehensive bibliography during 1936-1939 and 1946-1953. Additional information for the period before 1950 can be obtained from Gilbert Varet's *Manuel bibliographique de philosophie* (1956). The sections of the C.N.R.S. publication *Bulletin signalétique* which devoted to philosophy may also be useful, and provide abstracts.

Monographs, translations, pamphlets, and collections produced by Canadian philosophical authors can usually be traced through the various cumulations of the *National Union Catalogue* of the Library of Congress which includes some listings of library locations. Offprints of some review articles are also listed there. This catalogue is a main entry list, but provides cross references where an important author, editor, or translator does not appear in the first line of the main entry. The catalogues of the British Library and the Bibliothèque Nationale de France, *Canadiana* and the *Bibliographie du Québec* are also useful sources for information on monographs. What often cannot be located in such catalogues, however, are translations of items already published in English or French into other languages, especially non-European languages.

Philosophically relevant works that appear in predominantly theological sources can frequently be traced through the *Index to Religious Periodical Literature* (1949+, now *Religion Index I and Religion Index II*). General interest articles which appear in Catholic publications may be traced through the *Catholic Periodical Index* (1930+). Both sources index book reviews according to the author of the book reviewed and group them, in the most recent volumes, in separate sections. Many works in the Catholic tradition and on medieval philosophy can be tracked down through the *Bulletin thomiste* (1924-1967) and in the bibliographic issues of the *Revue d'histoire ecclésiastique* from Louvain. Philosophical articles which appear in scholarly journals not devoted principally to philosophy, or which appeared at periods predating the standard philosophical indexes, can be traced through the *International Index* (1907+), its predecessor, the *Cumulated Index to a Selected List of Periodicals* (1896+), and its successors, *The Humanities Index* and *The Social Science Index* (both 1974+). Articles in areas embraced by both philosophy and psychology can often be located through *Psychological Abstracts*, and especially through its cumulative author index. In some cases, references and abstracts for purely philosophical articles can be uncovered in this source. Works by Henry Wilkes Wright which appeared in such reviews as *Ethics* were discovered by this means. *L'Année philologique* (1925+) is useful for locating items in the history of classical philosophy in journals not indexed by, and in periods which predate, the standard philosophical indexes. The *Education Index* (1947+) and the *Canadian Education Index/Répertoire canadien sur l'education* (1965+) may be used to trace items in the philosophy of education which have appeared in reviews devoted to education. Philosophical articles published recently in some Quebec journals not elsewhere indexed can be located in *RADAR* (1972-83), and since 1983, in *Point de Repère* which has succeeded it and another index, *Périodex* (1972-83). Articles of philosophical relevance which appeared in non-academic Canadian periodicals can often be located by means of the *Canadian Periodical Index*.[14]

Location of works from the first four decades of this century and from the nineteenth century is a problem both for the bibliographer of philosophy and the bibliographer of Canadiana. There is a bibliographic dark age in both fields, especially for articles in scholarly journals.

Consider the Canadiana problem. There is no good index for periodicals in Canada for the period which predates the 1938-47 cumulative volume of the *Canadian Periodical Index*. An index covering the period 1920-38 has been prepared, but is not yet available. In addition, there is a very useful checklist of books and periodical articles on various subjects, including philosophy, which appeared in *Letters in Canada* between 1935 and 1941, after which that section of the *University of Toronto Quarterly* was restricted to a more general survey of Canadian letters and of writing in the humanities and the social sciences. *The Canadian Magazine* is indexed in the *Cumulated Index to a Selected List of Periodicals* and in the *International*

Index. Reviews such as the *Canadian Journal of Economics and Political Science* produced index volumes for their early years. Beyond that, however, the tracing of periodical items involves the tedious examination of the back files of reviews, or the reliance on already published bibliographies.[15] There is, however, a published index for one crucially important English Canadian periodical. That is Marilyn G. Flitton's, *An Index to the Canadian Monthly and National Review and to Rose Belford's Canadian Monthly and National Review 1872-1882.* (1976). In addition, during the early part of this century the *University of Toronto Monthly* published from time to time valuable lists of publications by faculty and by alumni. Publications such as the *Canadian Journal a*nd the *Christian Guardian* issued their own annual indexes.

Moreover, there are a few convenient sources of information for monographs and pamphlets. Bernard Amtmann's 4-volume *Short Title Catalogue of Canadiana* (1970-73), and Reginald E. Watter's *A Checklist of Canadian Literature 1628- 1960* (1959, 2 ed. 1972) provide both entries and library locations. *The Catalogue of Pamphlets in Public Archives* (1932) provides some assistance in locating short, often polemical, works. Since 1979, it has been supplemented by the general *Catalogue of the Public Archives Library/Catalogue de la Bibliothèque des Archives Publiques.* Henry J. Morgan's *Bibliotheca Canadensis* (1867 reprinted 1968) is an excellent bibliographic source for pre-confederation works, but very few works of any interest to philosophers are among them. The *Dictionnaire pratique des auteurs québécois* includes brief bibliographies for the authors listed as do several of the other standard Canadian biographic guides.

There are, of course, many other reference instruments for locating early Canadian writings. Most of these, however, are of only restricted use for those interested in the philosophical writing of the time. One may dip into them, but systematic use of all of them is time-consuming.

Nineteenth-century periodical articles in English can often be located by means of the *Wellesley Periodical Index* and by the much more extensive, but also more difficult to use, *Poole's Index to Periodical Literature* (1893-1938) along with the accompanying *Poole's Index: Date and Volume Key* by Marion Bell and Jean Bacon (1957). Bibliographic sources for philosophy during the nineteenth century tend, as they no doubt should, to focus on the noteworthy and readily accessible rather than on the obscure and hard to find.[16]

As to the period before the beginning of the nineteenth century, there is probably very little of philosophic interest to be found printed in Canada. Indeed there was very little of anything in print. There was, however, some teaching of philosophy, especially in Quebec, and there are some manuscript writings from the period.[17]

The bibliographic problem for the student of Canadian philosophy, then, is the location of nineteenth-century and twentieth-century sources. The items most difficult to locate using available instruments are articles in collections, translations of Canadian material, especially into non-European languages, and pre-1940 contributions to periodicals and newspapers. Only patient, first-hand searching of backfiles, the use of archives,[18] and extensive correspondence with others doing similar work can remedy these deficiencies.

Endnotes

1.See A. Brian McKillop *A Disciplined Intelligence.* (Montreal: McGill-Queen's, 1979), p.1-21.

2.Many would refuse to claim him as a philosopher. See Thomas Goudge, rev. of *Philosophy in the Mass Age, University of Toronto Quarterly,* Vol. 29 (JL 1960), p.486&7.

3.See McKillop pp. 206-228; Leslie Armour & Elizabeth Trott, *The Faces of Reason* (Waterloo, Ont.: Wilfrid Laurier University Press, 1981), p.269-360.

4.For a very negative but not unrealistic comment on the cultural impact of philosophy see the letter excerpt from O.D. Skelton to Adam Shortt, in Bryan Palmer's, *A Culture in Conflict* (Montreal: McGill-Queen's, 1979), p.236.

5.Claude Lévi-Strauss is one noteworthy example. See *Tristes Tropiques* (London: Atheneum, 1971), p.54-64.

6.See John M. MacEachran, "John Watson 1847-1939," in *Some Great Men of Queen's,* ed. by R.C. Wallace (Toronto: Ryerson 1940), p.22-50.

7.The rule of thumb which researchers were asked to employ before they deleted items on the ground of irrelevance was that they should be able to give a definite answer to the question, "If it isn't philosophy, what is it?"

8.Thus, even the anti-Catholic polemics of John Strachan, such as the *Poor Man's Preservative Against Popery* (Toronto: Bull, 1934) and tracts on education by Egerton Ryerson are included as examples of the sort of intellectual work current in early English Canada.

9.Albert-Marie Landry, "La pensée philosophique médiévale. Contribution canadienne (1960-1973)," *Philosophiques,* vol.1 (OC1974), p.111-39.

10.He was also a contributor to the *Canadian Monthly and National Review.* See McKillop, pp.157, 261.

11.Many of the instruments and techniques mentioned here are standard research tools, and can also be applied to other bio-bibliographic projects.

12.In addition, both Canadian and American philosophical journals, publishers, and societies are listed in the *Directory.*

13.Armour and Trott note that the philosophy department at the University of Toronto had seven members at the time of G.S. Brett's appointment and was the largest in Canada then. (*The Faces of Reason,* p.433) Careful examination shows, however, that five of these people were engaged in psychology.

14.Some authors with special concerns or special audiences may require additional searching in indexes appropriate to them. For example, in compiling a bibliography of Emil Fackenheim (See Part III, item 290), Mark Rabnett consulted the indexes to *Commentary, Conservative Judaism,* and *Judaism* as well as the *Index of Articles on Jewish Studies, the International Bibliography of Jewish Affairs,* and the *Index to Jewish Periodicals*.

15.Another source is the lucky discovery of extensive offprint collections in archives. Such a collection exists for H.L. Stewart in the Dalhousie University Archives.

16.Sometimes, however, Benjamin Rand's *Bibliography of Philosophy, Psychology and Cognate Subjects* (New York: Macmillan, 1905, 2 vols.; also appearing as Vol. 3, Parts 1 and 2 of Baldwin's *Dictionary of Philosophy and Psychology,* New York: Macmillan, 1905) is useful. For example, articles published on child psychology by James Mark Baldwin while he was at Toronto are listed in close proximity to articles published on the same subject shortly thereafter by Frederick Tracy of the same department. Anyone interested in the development of psychology from philosophy or in the sources of interest in child study at Toronto would find such information helpful.

17.See Yvon Lamonde, *La philosophie et son enseignement au Québec* (1665-1920) (Ville LaSalle: Hurtubise HMH, 1980) p.275-280 for a list.

18.In addition to the Dalhousie University Archives, archives and rare book collections at the University of Toronto (including those of the federated colleges), Queen's, McGill, and Manitoba should prove especially helpful for the historian of philosophic activities. In Quebec, special attention should be paid to the archives at Laval and the Université de Montréal. The Université d'Ottawa and the older classical colleges should also not be neglected.

Introduction

La discipline et son audience

Ce guide se divise en trois parties. La première partie est un guide général de techniques et d'instruments disponibles à ceux qui cherchent à faire de la recherche bibliographique sur les travaux de Canadiens en philosophie et en ses sujets alliés. La deuxième partie est une liste de sources importantes, soit bibliographiques, soit historiques, qui fournissent des renseignements sur la philosophie et ses sujets alliés produits au Canada. La troisième partie fournit des renseignements au sujet des oeuvres importantes publiées par les philosophes anglo-canadiens durnat la période avant 1950. Les remarques préliminaires servent à établir l'utilité des trois sections ainsi que l'utilité d'une bibliographie générale de la philosophie au Canada. De plus, une définition de la discipline est présentée et défendue.

Quoique la discipline de philosophie admette nombre de practiciens qui se contentent de maîtriser la littérature d'une section particulière de la discipline de façon non formelle, le succès des publications du Philosophy Documentation Center, et du *Philosophers Index* et de son service d'informatique en particulier, indique qu'à mesure que la communauté philosophique et ses intérèts se sont étendus et sont devenus plus complexes, des moyens d'accès plus organisés aux discussions publiques de problèmes philosophiques sont devenus de plus en plus appreciés. Une bibliographie générale de la philosophie au Canada profiterait à nombreux interessés de les philosophes. Les historiens de la vie intellectuelle la trouveraient avantageuse aussi.

Tous les philosophes au Canada trouveront dans cette bibliographie un recensement utile du travail de leurs collègues. Où l'intérèt se limite au travail contemporain, une bibliographie telle que celle-ci offrira un accès plus étendu aux matériaux déjà récupérables à travers le *Philosophers Index* et le *Répertoire bibliographique de la philosophie*. De plus elle sera peut-être mieux organisée pour certaines recherches--par auteurs, par exemple, plutôt que par années et ensuite par auteurs. Les philosophes qui s'intéressent aux problèmes historiques trouveront peut-être, dans cette bibliographie, de l'information sur des premiers penseurs canadiens qui n'est pas autrement récupérable sous forme bibliographique. Ce guide fournira le moyen d'assembler des références à des oeuvres, par et à propos de philosophes, qui n'apparaissent pas dans les index des oeuvres de fond des bibliographies courantes. Plusieurs des techniques présentées et quelques-uns des instruments peuvent aussi être généralisés en vue de fournir un guide pour d'autres projets bio-bibliographiques en philosophie et en ses sujets aliés.

Certains philosophes croient qu'il est important de réfléchir sur les traditions philosophiques qui existent dans les cultures du Canada-anglais et du Québec. Des réflexions historiques de ce genre pourraient illuminer la nature de la philosophie et indiquer si les cultures canadiennes ont produit quelque chose qui mériterait une place à l'agenda philosophique. A la base de ce raisonnement se trouvent peut-être des idées essentiellement idéalistes: une conviction que différentes cultures expriment et vivent les conséquences des idées et théories qui leur sont appropriées et que la philosophie constitue une partie importante de la réflexion d'une culture sur sa vie intellectuelle. A part, une base idéaliste, l'intention pourrait se fonder sur la conviction marxiste qui maintient qu'une philosophie ou groupe de philosophies dans une société reflètent et, à un moindre degré, réagissent aux conflits sociaux de la société. Si on espère suivre la pensée marxiste, il sera necessaire, premièrement, d'établir non seulement le genre de doctrines philosophiques qui existent dans la société mais aussi leur valeur, et, deuxièment, d'établir le lien entre ces philosophies et les conflits qui leur sont associés. Les philosophes qui sont attirés au travail des historicistes ou des relativistes trouveront une bibliographie générale utile aussi. Ils pourront s'en servir pour essayer de comprendre le caractère spécial de la contribution philosophique d'une nation. Si ces philosophes ne sont pas membres du groupe dont ils font l'étude, leurs buts seront essentiellement ethnologiques. Si par contre, ils se considèrent comme membres du groupe en question, leur étude représentera un effort pour se comprendre. L'historiciste voudra peut-être placer ses resultats dans un contexte plus large, le relativiste considérera la chose comme impossible. Quelques soient leurs buts ils devront identifier les oeuvres philosophiques produits par la société avant de caractériser sa philosophie 'nationale.'

Même ceux qui doutent que ce soit possible de décrire une philosophie nationale--ou un groupe de philosophies nationales--dans un état multi-nationale, trouveront peut-être dans les ressources présentées dans ce guide ou dans une bibliographie provenant de ce guide, les moyens de défendre leurs points de vue ou de mettre leurs adversaires en déroute.

Les philosophes ne sont pas les seuls à s'intéresser à un compte rendu des écrits philosophiques canadiens. Les historiens de la vie intellectuelle auront les bienfaits de l'accès à plusieurs des produits idéologiques les plus abstraits ou les plus généraux du pays. Bien que ces écrits n'aient peut-être pas exercés une très grande influence sur la vie quotidienne au moment de leur parution, ils peuvent conduire à des réflexions intéressantes sur l'état d'esprit ou les suppositions sous-jacentes de l'élite intellectuelle au moment en question. C'est justement dans leur nature abstraite et générale que se trouve le mérite de ces écrits. Eloignés de la spécificité des débats politiques et économiques de leur époque, ils ne sont pas aussi limités par des lignes de parti pris excessivement partisanes que le journalisme et les écrits économiques, politiques et même historiques de la période. La différence entre un chercheur en philosophie et un autre, et surtout entre un style ou un mouvement philosophique et un autre, pourrait également révéler des différences profondes dans la société en général.

Le genre d'information auquel ce guide donnera accès contribuera à la résolution de problèmes de nature historique. Le point de vue des intellectuels canadiens du dix-neuvième siècle était-il, contraire à celui des intellectuels américains, plutôt religieux et moraliste que sceptique ou critique?1 Est-ce que certains intellectuels ont fait preuve de différents niveaux de scepticisme ou de moralisme? Qu'est qui pourrait expliquer ces différences, ou les tendances qu'ils révèlent? L'existence de travaux bio-bibliographiques solides facilitera la tâche d'acquérir la connaissance approfondie de la littérature philosophique de l'époque nécessaire à la resolution de ces problèmes.

Grâce à ces travaux, on pourra établir un compte rendu plus complet des idées des philosophes canadiens concernant des sujets tels que l'importance de la science dans leur vie, ou encore, leurs convictions au sujet de la nature humaine et des bases de la moralité. On pourra déterminer également de quelle façon les points de vue de divers auteurs sont déterminés par leurs origines sociales et ethniques, de leur position sociale et celle du lecteur visé. Ceci permettra la mise à l'épreuve de diverses hypothèses sur l'histoire de la vie intellectuelle du pays.

De plus, il y a bon nombre de philosophes au Canada qui sont d'intérèt aux historiens pour des raisons autres que leur capacité de réfléchir sur de grandes idées sociales. Ici, il faudrait surtout noter les amateurs cultivés et les professionels éminents. Les premiers ne sont ni écrivains ni professeurs de philosophie de métier, mais ils abordent des sujets philosophiques-

-ou des sujets auxquels les philosophes s'intéressent--dans leurs poursuites intellectuelles. Parmi les membres de ce groupe se trouvent des intellectuels tels que William Dawson LeSueur et Goldwin Smith au Canada-anglais, et Etienne Parent au Québec. Quant au deuxième groupe, on y retrouve les philosophes dont les travaux ou les cours ont contribué à la formation des idées de ceux qui poursuivent des études dans d'autres domaines. A ce groupe figurent John Watson dont les opinions influencèrent les fondateurs de l'Eglise-Unie, George Parkin Grant[2], Charles DeKoninck, Louis-Adolphe Pâquet, et le Cardinal Villeneuve. De plus, il y a plusieurs philosophes importants dont le travail proprement philosophique ne représente qu'un aspect d'une carrière très variée. Parmi ces derniers pourraient figurer Emile Fackenheim et Francis Sparshott, François Hertel, et Jean LeMoyne. Il y a aussi des universitaires titulaires de chaires en disciplines autres que philosophie qui exercent leur influence principalement dans ces domaines mais qui ont fait d'importantes contributions aux études philosophiques. Sous cette rubrique on pourrait inclure C.B. Macpherson, John O'Neill, et Fernand Dumont.

Dans certains cas, des débats aux sous-entendus philosophiques ont accompagné d'importants développements historiques. Il en est définitement ainsi au Québec où l'apparition de--et l'opposition à--l'-Institut canadien, le développement de l'ultramontanisme et les disputes sur le libéralisme politique ont tous compris des aspects philosophiques et socio-politiques. Ces liens historio-philosophiques sont moins en évidence au Canada-anglais mais, même là, on a pu noter le rapprochement de certains genres d'idéalisme et d'impérialisme, et l'association étroite des courants idéalistes à la création de l'Eglise-Unie et au mouvement socio-evangélique.[3] Richard Maurice Bucke était un alieniste actif dans la mouvement pour réformes au bénéfice des aliénés. Ses efforts allaient de paire avec ses idées singulières sur le rapport entre la disposition morale et le système nerveux et avec des opinions au sujet des avantages adaptatifs de diverses dispositions.

Néanmoins, l'historien de la société s'interessera plus aux doctrines philosophiques en tant que réflexions et effets des conditions sociales qu'en tant que causes d'importants développements historiques. Les idées des philosophes ont un effet général seulement au moment ou plusieurs personnes sont prêtes à les accepter et à les utiliser. D'habitude, on arrive a cette acceptation publique seulement après que les idées ont filtré à travers plusieurs intermédiaires.[4]

Quels genres d'écrits le bibliographe doit-il considérer suffisamment philosophiques pour être inclus dans une bibliographie et récupérés par un guide? Aucune discipline académique a les bornes si claires que ses intérèts sont complètement isolés de ceux d'autres disciplines. Les bornes deviennent encore plus vagues lorsqu'on examine la discipline en diachronie. Le principe général le plus approprié aux bibliographies historiques semblerait être celui d'inclusion maximale justifiable.

Les travaux bibliographiques qui visent à donner accès à la philosophie canadienne doivent se montrer utiles aux historiens de la société qui possèdent des notions variées, et peut-être vagues, de la philosophie. Plusieurs s'intéresseront principalement aux liens entre ce qu'ils considèrent la philosophie et d'autres disciplines. Il n'y a plus aucun doute que les frontières de la discipline se sont déplacées. C'est un fait qu'admettent même ceux qui aimeraient limiter le terme 'philosophie' aux sujets généralement présentés dans les départements académiques de la philosophie. Les étudiants et les professeurs de la philosophie ont eux mêmes des opinions divergentes sur de la nature de leur discipline. C'est au bibliographe qui s'occupe de la préparation d'une bibliographie générale institutionelle de la philosophie, ou d'instruments voués à l'identification de travaux de la discipline, de fournir un instrument de recherche utile à tous les philosophes at aux historiens s'intéressant à un nombre de périodes d'histoire de la vie intellectuelle. Pour cette raison le bibliographe doit résister la tentation de limiter l'étendu de ses références.

En raison de ces problèmes, une bibliographie générale de la philosophie au Canada doit inclure des références à beaucoup de travaux de psychologie, discipline qui de nos jours est considérée indépendante de la philosophie. A l'University of Toronto on enseigna la psychologie en tant que branche de la philosophie au cours de la première partie de ce siècle. La psychologie fut enseignée conjointement avec la philosophie à Dalhousie et à l'University of British Columbia pendant encore plus longtemps et, jusqu'au milieu de ce siècle, à l'Université d'Ottawa et à l'Université de Montréal, le Département de Psychologie faisait encore part de la Faculté de Philosophie. Jusqu'au milieu des années soixante un cours préliminaire en psychologie figurait à la liste des cours de philosophie au St. Michael's College à l'University of Toronto. Même quelque années après sa suppression comme cours officiel de philosophie, il était toujours proposé comme cours actif au programme d'études. La longévité de ce cours reflétait la conviction de plusieurs philosophes versés dans la tradition catholique que la psychologie et les autres sciences humaines devraient se nourrir en partie de la philosophie. En raison de ce genre de réflexion, ce guide indiquera les instruments qui faciliteraient l'identification des contributions imprimées de ces premiers psychologues canadiens.

On peut aussi se servir de certains instruments pour localiser des rédactions qu'on pourraient appeler socio- scientifiques. Plusieurs pionniers des sciences sociales, tels que Adam Smith, John Stuart Mill, Max Weber et Emile Durkheim reçurent une formation philosophique. Au dix-neuvième siècle et au début du vingtième siècle, la philosophie au Canada-anglais était encore étroitement liée aux travaux en sciences sociales. Un nombre d'érudits éminents contemporains du monde des sciences sociales furent recrutés des rangs des philosophes.[5] Au Québec le développement de départements autonomes de diverses sciences sociales date de l'après-guerre. A Queen's, une université de tradition écossaise, au dix-neuvième siècle on assignait souvent des cours voués à des sujets tels que l'économie politique aux titulaires d'une chaire en philosophie.[6] Même de nos jours, les universitaires dont la specialité est étroitement liée aux recherches socio-scientifiques, telles que la théorie des jeux et la théorie des décisions, influencèrent beaucoup la philosophie au Canada-anglais. Par conséquent, certains écrits qu'on pourrait considérer comme exposés généraux de la théorie socio-scientifique seront inclus dans notre bibliographie de la philosophie au Canada.

Ainsi le bibliographe doit considérer des oeuvres provenant d'autres domaines particulierement quand certains philosophes, du présent ou du passé, les jugent essentiel à leurs travaux philosophiques. Aucun jugement qui portesur la qualité du travail ne doit influencer la décision d'en tenir compte dans la bibliographie. Tout comme l'archéologue qui, dans son enquête sur l'art céramique d'une société, tient compte à la fois de bons et de mauvais échantillons, le bibliographe doit cataloguer les écrits de mauvaise qualité en même temps que les chefs-d'oeuvres intellectuels.

Une bibliographie qui suit ces principes sera, sans aucun doute, très vaste. Organisée par auteurs, elle fournira un guide qui répondra aux besoins du chercheur qui s'intéresse a un individu en particulier. Des routes d'accès supplémentaires faciliteront sa tâche. Si on assigne un nombre de vedettes matières à chaque notice et si on fournit des moyens de repérer les documents par date et langue de publication, la tâche de localiser de l'information sera largement simplifiée. La bibliographie qui résulterait de l'usage des techniques et des instruments de ce guide permettrait une telle recupération d'information. De plus, les instruments et techniques présentés dans la première partie faciliteront la rédaction de bibliographies plus spécialisées. A vrai dire, un bon nombre de ces bibliographies spécialisées figurent à la liste de contrôle des matériaux de recherche dans la deuxième partie de cet ouvrage.

Une bibliographie générale de la philosophie au Canada comprendra, par conséquent, plusieurs notices d'oeuvres qui ne sont pas proprement

philosophiques mais qui semblent également refuser toute autre rubrique.[7]
Une telle bibliographie comprendra des oeuvres avec très peu de contenu
philosophique qui, néanmoins, sont des exemples de ce qui précéda et qui
prépara le terrain intellectuel pour les écrits qui sont considérés comme
plus philosophiques.[8] On tiendra compte également des travaux des "non-
philosophes" qui influencèrent soit les philosophes même, soit le milieu
intellectuel des philosophes. Par conséquent, certains écrits des
théoriciens de la communication, Harold Innis et Marshall McLuhan,
trouveront une place dans la bibliographie. De façon semblable, des études
qui traitent de personnages historiques dont le travail intéressera les
chercheurs de plusieurs disciplines doit être inclues. La bibliographie
comprendra donc des discussions d'importance théologique sur saint
Augustin, sur Thomas d'Aquin ou sur saint Bonaventure également, des
études littéraires sur Nietzsche, des études théologiques sur Kierkegaard
et des analyses des aspects "philosophiques" des écrits de Newton, de
Darwin, d'Einstein et de Durkheim. On inclura aussi les travaux d'auteurs
qui sont actifs dans des disciplines limitrophes; par exemple, beaucoup
d'écrits savants de G.M.A. Grube un classiciste de Toronto méritent une
place dans notre bibliographie. Finalement, on tiendra compte des travaux
non-philosophiques des philosophes canadiens lorsqu'ils servent à
déterminer l'influence de la philosophie sur d'autres domaines. C'est pour
cette raison qu'on se devra d'inclure des études sur le Credit-social en
Alberta par John Irving et par C.B. Macpherson.

   Il y a trois règles qu'on peut suivre lorsqu'il s'agit de déterminer si des
travaux considérés comme "philosophiques" sont également "canadiens."
La première règle considére ceux qui s'intéressent à la philosophie dans un
pays spécifique, à un moment précis, comme membres d'une communauté
qui produit et consomme des écrits philosophiques. On pourrait mesurer
le développement de la communauté au cours d'une année donnée en
recensant les écrits produits et consommés. Cependant, une bibliographie
qui comprendrait beaucoup de travaux écrits et publiés en Ecosse ou en
France ou aux Etats-Unis (ou en Allemagne ou en Grèce antique) par les
citoyens de ces pays ne répondraient pas à l'attente des chercheurs qui
s'attendent à un bibliographie de la philosophie canadienne, bien qu'un
compte rendu de ce qui fut lu ou commenté par les étudiants et par les
praticiens en philosophie--ou un recensement du contenu de leurs
bibliothèques--occupe, sans aucun doute, une place importante dans
l'histoire de la discipline et de la communauté philosophique.

   Il y a beaucoup d'arguments en faveur de l'inclusion de tout écrit
canadien et de tout écrit publié au Canada. Quelques bibliographies, dont
celle de Landry qui recense les contributions canadiennes à la philosophie

médiévale, suivent cette règle.[9] On pourrait suggérer que la création d'une liste des publications philosophiques des éditeurs canadiens faciliterait la création d'un portrait de l'état de la communauté philosophique car elle aiderait les universitaires à mesurer l'importance et l'impact international de la communauté (on pourrait soutenir qu'une communauté est importante lorsqu'elle comprend des maisons d'édition qui font paraître une grande variété de travaux rédigés par des collaborateurs étrangers), et donner un aperçu de ce qui est et fut produit pour le marché domestique.

Cette première règle d'inclusion n'est pas sans faiblesse. En raison des lois sur les droits d'auteurs ou simplement parce que c'est plus commode, certains livres publiés au Canada sont distribués par des filiales canadiennes d'éditeurs internationales. Dans d'autres cas, en conséquence d'accords de droits entre des éditeurs canadien et des éditeurs à l'étranger, on observe parmi la production 'canadienne' plusieurs éditions de livres importants internationaux dont seule la page de titre sert à différencier l'édition canadienne de l'édition de l'éditeur principal.

Quelques articles de revue s'avèrent également trompeurs. Bien que l'existence de revues specialisées tels que *Mediaeval Studies* indique un niveau très élevé de développement académique au Canada, ces revues sont surtout destinées à un public étranger. Un article dans une telle revue rédigé par un Allemand pour des lecteurs dispersés un peu partout en Europe et aux Amériques ne reflètera pas très bien l'activité philosophique proprement canadienne, même si, parmi ces lecteurs, se trouvaient quelques Canadiens. De plus, il y a des revues qui ne représentent qu'un simple violon d'ingre de l'éditeur. Si un éditeur-professeur accepte un poste académique au Canada, il est probable que sa revue l'accompagnera pendant son séjour, quoique ce séjour soit de courte durée. La revue *Telos*, par exemple, est inextricablement lié à Paul Piccone qui pendant quelque temps fut attaché au Département de Sociologie à l'University of Toronto. Pourtant, cette association de courte durée n'a 'canadienniser' ni la revue ni ses collaborateurs non-canadiens.

De nos jours, les périodiques canadiens remplissent un autre rôle qui pose des problèmes à cette première règle. On fait pression sur les universitaires pour qu'ils publient des articles. En ce qui concerne la philosophie, les périodiques importants de l'Amérique anglophone refusent jusqu'à 90 per cent des articles reçus. Comme résultat, beaucoup d'auteurs font circuler leurs manuscrits un peu partout dans le monde anglophone, les faisant parvenir aux revues qui ne sont peut-être pas de qualité inférieure, mais qui sont de second ordre aux yeux des praticiens. Même les revues qui s'addressent aux lecteurs d'un pays ou d'une région précise sont destinataires de ces manuscrits. Les revues canadiennes semblent appartenir à ce groupe et servent souvent de débouchés pour des philosophes étrangers.

Bien que les revues canadiennes (parmi d'autres) soient récemment devenues des débouchés commodes pour certains écrivains étrangers, un tout autre phenomène trompeur existe depuis plusieurs décennies. La revue intellectuelle du dix-neuvième siècle désirait ardemment des écrits qui satisferaient des lecteurs à la fois spécialistes et amateurs de diverses disciplines. Dans quelques régions, dont le Canada-anglais en particulier, la demande pour ces écrits depassait parfois l'offre. Une solution qui se présentat aux rédacteurs des revues en question fut de solliciter ou même de réimprimer des articles venus d'ailleurs. Cette solution était d'autant plus attirante lorsque ces écrits provenaient d'endroits qui se vantaient d'être d'une superiorité culturelle. Plusieurs articles qui ont paru dans le *Canadian Monthly and National Review* parvenaient de sources anglaises. Quelques articles, tels que ceux de George John Romanes, étaient rédigés par des Canadiens de naissance qui avaient acquis une certaine renommée en Grande-Bretagne.[10] D'autres articles étaient simplement des écrits d'auteurs qui traitaient des matières que les éditeurs croyaient d'intérèt aux Canadiens instruits. Ce genre de contribution étrangère indique que la communauté intellectuelle d'une région n'a pas encore atteint l'indépendance, et qu'elle demeure coloniale. L'existence des écrits de ce genre est très importante et mérite certainement une place dans les livres d'histoire mais leurs présence dans une bibliographie générale pourrait être trompeuse.

La deuxième façon d'aborder le problème de la documentation de la discipline serait de ne tenir compte que des écrits des auteurs canadiens. Le bibliographe se transformerait en archéologue de la litterature et cataloguerait tout produit ou toute trace des outils d'un certain genre d'industrie intellectuelle. Cette stratégie est beaucoup plus restrictive que la première, parce que elle ne tient pas compte de plusieurs écrits qui sont bibliographiquement trompeurs. Elle passe sous silence aussi des articles qu'on souhaiterait inclure. Elle exclut, par exemple, les textes importés qui influencèrent les attitudes des philosophes et du public instruit: l'-*Institutiones*, employé au Québec et aux collèges catholiques du Canada-anglais, et les écrits de Paley, Bain, et McCosh utilisés dans le reste du Canada-anglais. Elle n'inclurerait pas non plus les grands travaux importés qui eurent un impact important et qui générèrent beaucoup de discussion sans provoquer de commentaires écrits. Cette façon d'aborder le problème risque également d'exclure les écrits des expatriés très influents qui n'ont pas eu de carrière professionelle au Canada. Une bibliographie générale peut servir l'historien mais il n'est pas nécessaire ni qu'elle remplace ses efforts descriptifs.

Un catalogue d'oeuvres intellectuels ne fournit pas le moyen de juger l'importance relative des articles reunis. On voudrait savoir si des Canadiens qui ont produit des idées philosophiques étaient, en réalité, membres d'une communauté où avaient lieu beaucoup d'échanges ou un groupe d'intellectuels isolés, chacun travaillant indépendemment de ses homologues, et possédant ses propres lecteurs. Le bibliographe peut fournir des renseignements sur l'importance générale d'un travail en recensant les réimpressions, les nouvelles éditions et les traductions où elles sont repérables. L'étendue géographique de l'influence d'un auteur peut être mesurée en partie en faisant le recensement des oeuvres de l'auteur qui furent publiés hors Canada. On peut établir la nature de la communauté intellectuelle dans laquelle se place l'auteur en examinant les commentaires publiés sur ces travaux.

La troisième règle d'inclusion prévoit non seulement le recensement de tous les auteurs canadiens mais encore l'incorporation de tous les com-mentaires sur ces auteurs. Ceci est la règle adoptée par la Bibliographie de la Philosophie au Canada dont les chercheurs ont catalogué, en même temps que les sources premières, les écrits des Canadiens au sujet d'autres Canadiens, notant l'auteur dont il est question ainsi que le recenseur afin de mesurer l'ampleur du réseau de contacts entre philosophes canadiens.

Il faut toutefois reconnaître que cette règle d'inclusion n'est pas sans limites. Il est difficile de fournir une liste complète de traductions, de réimpressions, de nouvelles éditions, et de commentaires. Ce n'est qu'au moyen d'indexes déjà en existence, des vedettes matiéres des catalogues dans les bibliothèques, et de certaines ressources canadiennes classiques, mais limitées, de renseignements bibliographiques qu'on peut recupérer les écrits au sujet d'auteurs canadiens. Les traductions en langues non-européennes s'avèrent difficile à retrouver, particulièrement les plus an-ciennes. Il ne serait possible ni de tenir compte de toutes les réimpressions de livres populaires, ni d'établir l'étendue de chaque impression. Les nouvelles éditions et, en particulier, les nouvelles éditions de traductions, échappent souvent à tout effort de recensement.

Ce qu'on trouvera pour représenter chaque auteur se modifiera selon un réseau complexe de facteurs. Parfois ces facteurs seront systématiques (Quelle est l'époque pendant laquelle l'auteur a produit la majorité de ses oeuvres? Quelles périodes sont recensées dans les indexes?), certains facteurs seront strictement personnels (Qui a fourni le classement par sujet du *Philosopher's Index* pour les articles publiés dans une revue en particulier au cours d'une année donnée?). Il n'est même pas possible, donc, de suggérer que les écrits recensés dans les sources bibliographiques représentent un pourcentage uniforme des oeuvres dans cette catégorie. Ainsi, tout ce qu'on peut tirer d'une bibliographie organisée à la manière de la B.P.C. sont des suggestions plutôt que des indications précises de l'importance d'un auteur. Ces suggestions indiquent, pourtant, l'influence minimale de chaque auteur, et elles pourraient s'avérer utiles à l'historien de la vie intellectuelle. Les commentaires et les revisions notées pourraient également servir l'historien de la philosophie.

Première Partie

Guide de la recherche sur l'histoire de la philosophie au Canada

Ceux qui cherchent à rédiger une bibliographie qui se rapporte spécifiquement à une discipline ou sous-discipline font face à deux problèmes. Ils doivent d'abord dresser et vérifier une liste des auteurs qui ont écrit sur les sujets auxquels se voue la bibliographie. Ils doivent ensuite dresser et vérifier une liste des écrits pertinents de ces mêmes auteurs. Les techniques et les instruments bibliographiques qu'on présentera dans cette section faciliteront la résolution des problèmes que confrontent les Canadiens qui travaillent en philosophie ou dans une discipline associée.[11]

Comment peut-on identifier les Canadiens qui ont effectué des travaux en philosophie? De nos jours, les philosophes préfèrent l'université comme habitat. Le plus souvent on peut repérer le philosophe dans un département de philosophie universitaire ou au sein des listes de membres de diverses associations philosophiques. On peut consulter les annuaires universitaires et la liste des membres de l'Association Canadienne de Philosophie pour déterminer les philosophes actifs à une époque quelconque. Ce genre de renseignement peut s'avérer difficile à retrouver dans un seul endroit mais, pour certaines périodes, il existe des raccourcis qui peuvent faciliter la tâche.

Le *Directory of American Philosophers* énumère les philosophes canadiens qui donnent des cours dans les instituts recensés. On peut y avoir recours pour se renseigner au sujet de ceux qui participent à l'enseignement philosophique et pour obtenir une impression de l'ampleur et de la composition d'une telle ou telle faculté. L'énumération par le *Directory* énumère aussi des étudiants du deuxième ou du troisième cycle peut être à la fois utile et déroutant.[12]

Une autre oeuvre utile est le *Directory of American Scholars* rédigé en quatre tomes qui comprend des biographies de plusieurs philosophes canadiens (aussi bien que celles d'auteurs en lettres) et un index général. Cet instrument a déjà été réédité plusieurs fois, le plus récemment en 1985. Ce travail ne tient compte que des universitaires actifs et de ceux qui viennent tout juste d'abandonner la philosophie; il faut donc vérifier dans les numéros antécédents les noms de ceux qui sont décédés ou retraités. Quoique nulle édition ne soit parfaitement complète, même à l'égard des personnes qui enseignaient activement au moment de l'impression du numéro, les esquisses biographiques fournissent beaucoup de details sur l'histoire et sur les intérèts académiques de chaque individu particulièrement a l'égard de sa nationalité on sa specialité académique. On peut trouver une liste des corps enseignants des universités du Commonwealth dans le *Commonwealth Universities Yearbook*. Cet annuaire s'avère très utile en ce qui concerne l'époque qui a précédé l'apparition d'autres répertoires. Les listes d'adhérents de l'Association Canadienne de Philosophie fournissent des renseignements non seulement au sujet de nombreux membres de départements de philosophie mais encore de philosophes qui ne sont pas titulaires de postes universitaires.

Les histoires des ordres religieux, les histoires de divers universités et collèges, les rapports du président des universités, les archives universitaires et les histoires des départements de philosophie et d'autres départements associés représentent également des sources sûres. Une sélection de ces sources sera présentée dans la deuxième partie de cet exposé. Quand on a affaire à des histoires et à des rapports de département publiés dans des sources telles que le *Commonwealth Universities Yearbook*, il faut prendre soin de noter l'existence des facultés de philosophie qui ont plusieurs départements. Jusqu'à très recemment ces facultés multi-dimensionelles existaient à l'Université de Montréal et à l'Université d'Ottawa. Ces facultés peuvent posséder des départements de psychologie, d'études médiévales et de pédagogie. Une référence à un professeur de la faculté de philosophie d'un tel institut doit être vérifiée pour déterminer si l'individu donnait en realité, des cours de philosophie ou s'il travaillait dans une matière apparentée. De la même manière, les premiers départements de philosophie de certaines universités, dont l'-University of Toronto, comptaient les psychologues parmi leur nombre. On doit donc agir avec circonspection pour déterminer si, oui ou non, les membres de certains départements conforment aux catégories à l'usage aujourd'hui.[13]

Le *Literary History of Canada* de Karl Klinck est une autre source précieuse de renseignements sur des philosophes. La première édition et l'édition en trois volumes récemment mise à jour offrent des chapitres sur les écrits philosophiques au Canada. De plus, il y a des chapitres sur les belles-lettres et sur les écrits dans le domaine de la théologie, des sciences sociales et des sciences naturelles qui fournissent des renseignements sur des auteurs qui chevauchent un nombre de disciplines.

Il existe plusieurs moyens d'établir l'identité des personnes citées comme philosophes dans les sources de base. Une fois qu'on a établi la date de décès d'un auteur du dix-neuvième siècle, on peut dépouiller les volumes du *Dictionnaire biographique du Canada* pour obtenir des détails biographiques. Les renseignements sur çeux qui sont décédes en dehors des periodes recensées par cette source peuvent être vérifiés grâce au *Macmillan Dictionary of Canadian Biography* de William Stewart Wallace. Le *Canadian Who's Who et Canadian Men and Women of the Time* de Henry J. Morgan (1898 et 1912) peuvent également s'avérer utiles. Pour confirmer la nationalité des philosophes plus récents, on peut consulter l'-*International Directory of Philosophy and Philosophers*, liste comprehensive des philosophes et des instituts philosophiques en dehors de l'Amérique du nord (l'édition la plus recente date de 1986-89). Quant aux biographies des savants en sciences naturelles et en sciences sociales qui s'intéressent également aux questions philosophiques, on peut les identifier avec l'aide de diverses éditions de *American Men and Women of Science* et de son prédécesseur *American Men of Science*. Dans le *Dictionnaire pratique des auteurs québécois* de Reginald Hamel, John Hare, et Paul Wyczynski (1976) se trouvent de courtes biographies d'importants auteurs québécois ainsi que des bibliographies concises.

Dans le cas où la nationalité ou la durée de séjour d'un philosophe sont en question, on peut quelquefois résoudre le problème en consultant des sources biographiques étrangères. Parmi les sources de Grande-Bretagne dignes d'attention figurent l'*Academic Who's Who*, le *Who was Who*, le *Who's Who* et le *Dictionary of National Biography*. Ces sources se montrent très utiles lorsqu'il s'agit de retrouver les Canadiens importants qui s'expatrièrent pendant longtemps. Le *Who's Who in America* et le *Who was Who* américain, ainsi que divers répertoires de biographie américains (e.g., *The National Cyclopedia of American Biography*, *The Dictionary of American*

Biography) s'avèrent précieux. Des *Who's Who* régionaux et spécialisés sont également utiles. On peut aussi avoir recours aux *Who's Who* français, espagnol, hollandais et allemand (*Wer ist Wer*), et à plusieurs guides historiques de la littérature française.

Au Québec et dans plusieurs instituts catholiques du Canada-anglais on compte beaucoup d'ecclésiastiques parmi ceux qui traitent de sujets philosophiques. On peut repérer des renseignements biographiques sur ces ecclésiastiques dans quelques sources spéciales. Diverses éditions du *Canada ecclésiastique* peuvent aider à situer des prêtres géographiquement au moment de la parution du répertoire. Les prêtres canadiens-français actifs avant 1936 figurent très souvent dans le *Dictionnaire biographique du clergé canadien- français* (1910+, 6 vols.) de Jean-Baptiste-Arthur Allaire. Les biographies des membres décédés canadiens de l'ordre des Oblats de Marie-Immaculée se trouvent dans les trois volumes du *Dictionnaire biographique des Oblats de Marie-Immaculée au Canada* (1976) de Gaston Carrière, et les noms des Basiliens décédés sont inscrits au *Dictionary of Basilian Biography* de Robert Scollard.

Une fois qu'on a repéré les philosophes, il reste à dresser la liste du leurs oeuvres. La technique de recherche nécessaire pour réaliser une telle liste diffère selon l'époque. Il est facile de dresser une liste vaste, quoique incomplète, des écrits philosophiques des années récentes. Les deux sources principales sont le *Philosopher's Index*, provenant du Philosophy Documentation Center à Bowling Green, Ohio, et le *Répertoire bibliographique de la philosophie* publié à Louvain. Le premier fut lancé en 1967 et comprend actuellement un index d'auteurs avec des synthèses de plusieurs articles, un vaste index de matières, un index de comptes rendus et des listes de traductions. On y indexe des revues en plusieurs langues mais les publications de langue anglaise prédominent. Le *Philosopher's Index* est accompagné de deux séries de tomes rétrospectifs qui embrassent la période de 1940 à 1966 pour les revues et la période de 1940 à 1976 pour les livres. La première série de tomes documente les publications de langue anglaise aux Etats-Unis. La deuxième série est un catalogue de toutes les autres publications anglophones non-américaines. Il y a un index d'auteurs avec quelques synthèses et un vaste index de matières. Les comptes rendus n'apparaissent que lorsqu'ils sont très importants. Le *Philosopher's Index* s'avère utile quand il s'agit de retrouver les écrits selon le sujet traité et se montre efficace mais quelque peu limité lorsqu'il faut retrouver les oeuvres d'un auteur.

Le *Répertoire bibliographique de la philosophie* ne se prête pas aussi facilement aux recherches selon une matière mais sa liste d'auteurs est moins limitée. Lancé en 1949, il succède aux numéros bibliographiques de la *Revue philosophique de Louvain* et à ceux du *Tijdschrift voor filosofie* tout en s'organisant de la même manière. Il fut crée dans le dessein de fournir un index compréhensif aux publications philosophiques en anglais, français, allemand, italien, espagnol, portugais, hollandais et catalan. Il fournit également quelques renseignements sur des articles écrits en d'autres langues européennes. Il catalogue des articles académiques, des opuscules, des monographies, et le contenu de certains mélanges et Festschriften. Les notices sont groupées sous des rubriques de sujet générales et on trouve un index d'auteurs à la fin du dernier tome de chaque année. Cette table onomastique permet au lecteur de retrouver non seulement les écrits d'un auteur, mais encore les comptes rendus de ces écrits et les commentaires sur l'auteur. Le dernier numéro annuel fournit également une liste des comptes rendus catalogués au cours de l'année, organisée par ordre alphabetique selon l'auteur du livre recensé ou selon le titre du livre recensé lorsqu'il n'y a pas d'auteur en particulier. Le *Répertoire* est la source la plus utile disponible à ceux qui voudraient composer une bibliographie des travaux philosophiques, publiés depuis la deuxième guerre mondiale, dans tous les domaines, à l'exception des études techniques en logique mathématique. Il est d'autant plus important qu'il énumère des publications en plusieurs langues qui sont parues avant 1967 et qu'il fournit des détails sur le contenu de beaucoup de mélanges. Les articles, soit nouvellement publiés, soit reimprimés, qui font partie de collections tels que des anthologies, des Festschriften ou des travaux publiés des congrès sont peut-être les écrits les plus difficiles à retrouver. On peut également avoir recours au *Répertoire* pour dresser une liste de comptes rendus rédigés par tel ou tel auteur. Cependant, la démarche à suivre pour aboutir à une telle liste s'avère compliquée et minutieuse. Il vous est vivement conseiller de vous reporter à l'introduction du travail avant d'entamer de telles recherches.

On peut parfois localiser des articles qui font partie de collections grâce à la *Bibliographie de la philosophie* qui, depuis 1954, recense des monographies et contient des abstraits de leur contenu. Les abstraits et les index d'auteurs, de collaborateurs, de traducteurs et de redacteurs mentionnés dans les abstraits peuvent fournir le nom de certains collaborateurs qu'on ne retrouve pas ailleurs. D'autres contributions à des mélanges d'écrits philosophiques peuvent parfois être recupérées grâce à *Essay and General Literature Index* (1900+), à travers *Canadian Book Review Annual* (1975+) et, plus rarement, dans *Canadian Essays and Collections Index 1971-2.*

Au *Répertoire* et à son prédécesseur s'ajoute le *Bibliographia Philosophica*, publication louvaniste de G.A. DeBrie, qui est organisé de la même façon que le *Répertoire* et qui couvre la période de 1934 à 1945. La période qui va du milieu des années trente à 1949 est couverte également par les prédecesseurs du *Répertoire* et par la *Bibliographie de la philosophie*, qui fut une bibliographie générale, peu compréhensive, pendant les années 1936-39 et 1946-53. Des renseignements supplémentaires sur la période antérieure à 1950 se trouvent dans le *Manuel bibliographique de philosophie* de Gilbert Varet (1956). Les sections du *Bulletin signalétique* qui traitent de la philosophie peuvent s'avérer également utiles et, de plus, contiennent des synthèses.

D'habitude on peut retrouver les monographies, les traductions, les opuscules et les mélanges rédigés par des philosophes canadiens au moyen de diverses éditions du *National Union Catalogue* de la Library of Congress, publication qui sert aussi a repérer les écrits moins connus. On peut aussi y trouver des tirés à part de quelques articles. Ce catalogue est une liste de notices principales, mais des renvois sont fournis lorsqu'il s'agit d'un auteur, d'un éditeur ou d'un traducteur important qui ne figure pas à la tête de la notice principale. *Canadiana, Bibliographie du Québec* et les catalogues de la British Library et de la Bibliothèque nationale de France sont aussi de bonnes sources de renseignements sur les monographies. Malheureusement, ces catalogues ne tiennent souvent pas compte des traductions en d'autres langues, surtout en langues non-européennes, d'ouvrages publiés antérieurement en anglais ou en français.

Des écrits philosophiques provenant de sources principalement théologiques peuvent être repérés grâce à l'*Index to Religious Periodical Literature* (1949+, actuellement le *Religion Index I* et le *Religion Index II*). On peut retrouver des articles d'intérèt général qui apparaissent dans les publications catholiques grâce au *Catholic Periodical Index* (1930+). Les deux sources indexent les comptes rendus selon l'auteur du livre recensé et les organisent, dans les derniers tomes, en sections distinctes. Avec l'aide du *Bulletin thomiste* (1924-1967) et des numéros bibliographiques de la *Revue d'histoire ecclésiastique* de Louvain, on peut répérer plusieurs écrits dans la tradition catholique et sur la philosophie médiévale. Les articles philosophiques qui apparaissent dans des revues académiques qui ne se vouent pas principalement à la philosophie, ou qui apparaissent à une date antérieure à la publication des grands index philosophiques, peuvent être récupérés au moyen de l'*International Index* (1907+), de son antecédent, le *Cumulated Index to a Selected List of Periodicals* (1896+), et de ses successeurs, le *Humanities Index* et le *Social Science Index* (1974+ dans les deux cas). Les articles qui chevauchent la philosophie et la psychologie peuvent souvent être répérés grâce au *Psychological Abstracts*, et plus particulièrement au moyen de son index cumulatif d'auteurs. Parfois on déterre de cette source des références et des synthèses d'articles purement philosophiques. C'est ainsi que le Projet a découvert des écrits de Henry Wilkes Wright qui furent publiés dans des périodiques tels que *Ethics*. *L'Année philologique* (1925+) s'avère utile en ce qui concerne les articles qui traitent de l'histoire de la philosophie classique dans les revues qui ne sont pas recensées par les indexes traditionnels voués à matières philosophiques soit à cause de leur date, soit à cause de leur contenu. On peut se servir de l'*Education Index* (1947+) et le *Canadian Education Index/Répertoire canadien sur l'éducation* (1965+) pour repérer des articles sur la philosophie d'éducation qui apparaissent dans des revues consacrées à l'éducation. Des articles philosophiques publiés récemment dans les revues québécoises qui ne sont pas recensés ailleurs se retrouvent dans *RADAR* (1972-83) et, depuis 1983, dans *Point de Repère* qui a succédé *RADAR* et *Périodex* (1972-83). Le *Canadian Periodical Index* est une source précieuse quand il s'agit d'identifier des articles philosophiques parus dans des revues non-académiques.[14]

Le bibliographe qui s'occupe de la philosophie et le bibliographe à la recherche de travaux canadiens éprouvent souvent de la difficulté à retrouver les écrits du dix-neuvième siècle et des quatre premières décennies de ce siècle. Ce sont des époques de ténèbres bibliographiques, surtout en ce qui concerne les revues savantes.

Considérons le problème des écrits canadiens. Il n'y a aucun bon index des revues au Canada pour la période antérieure à celle couverte par le tome cumulatif 1938-1947 du *Canadian Periodical Index*. Un index qui couvre la période de 1920 à 1938 fut complété mais n'a pas encore vu le jour. De plus, il existe une excellente liste de contrôle des livres et des articles où l'on aborde divers sujets, y compris la philosophie, dans la série *Letters in Canada* qui paru entre 1935 et 1941, et qui devint ensuite, dans l'*University of Toronto Quarterly*, un recensement plus général des lettres canadiennes et des études des belles lettres et des sciences sociales. L'-*International Index* indexe le *Canadian Magazine*. Certains revues telles que le *Canadian Journal of Economics and Political Science* dressèrent leur propre index pour recenser les articles de leurs premiers numéros. A part de ces sources, lorsqu'il est question de recupérer des articles, la recherche bibliographique nécessite un examen minutieux d'anciens numéros de revues ou une très grande dépendence sur des bibliographies.[15] Il y a cependant un *Index to the Canadian Monthly and National Review and to Rose Belford's Canadian Monthly and National Review 1872-1882* (The Bibliographical Society of Canada, 1976) de Marilyn G. Flitton qui tient compte du contenu d'un journal canadien-anglais de très grande importance. De plus, au début du vingtième siècle l'*University of Toronto Monthly* publia de temps à autre des listes d'oeuvres des membres des facultés de l'université et de ses gradués, et certaines revues, telles que le *Canadian Journal* et le *Christian Guardian*, publièrent un index annuel.

Il existe également quelques inventaires très utiles où on peut retrouver des renseignements sur des monographies et des opuscules. Le *Short Title Catalogue of Canadiana* de Bernard Amtmann en quatre volumes (1970-1973) et le *Checklist of Canadian Literature 1628-1960* de Reginald E. Watters (1959, 2 ième ed. 1972) fournissent à la fois des notices bibliographiques et des renseignements sur les bibliothèques où on peut retrouver les oeuvres. Le *Catalogue of Pamphlets in the Public Archives* (1932) se montre utile quand il s'agit de repérer des écrits très brefs qui sont souvent de nature polémique. Depuis 1979, il existe un catalogue plus générale, le *Catalogue of the Public Archives Library/Catalogue de la bibliothèque des archives publiques*.

La *Bibliotheca Canadensis* de Henry J. Morgan (1867, réimprimée 1968) demeure une bonne source bibliographique des ouvrages antérieurs à la Confédération, mais on y trouve très peu d'articles d'intérèt philosophique. Le *Dictionnaire pratique des auteurs québécois* de même que quelques autres guides classiques de la biographie canadienne comprennent des bibliographies concises des auteurs recensés.

Il existe, bien sur, plusieurs autres guides aux premiers écrits canadiens. En ce qui concerne les interessés de la philosophie, la plupart de ces sources sont d'une utilité limitée. Un dépouillement systematique de tels guides est possible mais prendrait beaucoup de temps.

On peut souvent repérer les articles des périodiques anglophones du dix-neuvième siècle au moyen du *Wellesley Periodical Index* et d'un travail plus complet mais plus difficile à utiliser, *Poole's Index to Periodical Literature* (1893-1938) et son volume compagnon, le *Poole's Index: Date and Volume Key* de Marion Bell et de Jean Bacon (1957). Les sources bibliographiques consacrées à la philosophie du dix-neuvième siècle ont tendance, avec raison sans doute, à concentrer leur attention sur les travaux importants et accessibles plutôt que sur ceux qui sont obscurs et difficiles à repérer.[16]

En ce qui concerne la période antérieure au dix-neuvième siècle, il n'y a probablement pas beaucoup d'écrits canadiens d'intérèt philosophique à repérer--à vrai dire il n'y a pas beaucoup d'écrits canadiens sur quoi que ce soit. Avant 1800, on proposait quelques cours de philosophie, surtout au Québec, dont on a gardé la trace grâce aux manuscrits de l'époque.[17]

Le plus grand problème bibliographique auquel l'étudiant de la philosophie canadienne fait face est de repérer des sources du dix-neuvième et du vingtième siècle. Les travaux qui s'avèrent le plus difficiles à repérer sont les articles qui font partie des mélanges, la traduction des écrits canadiens, surtout en langues non-européenes, et les contributions aux journaux et aux revues d'avant 1940. Ce n'est qu'à travers un examen minutieux d'anciens numéros, l'emploi des archives,[18] et un vaste reseau de correspondence avec ceux qui s'occupent du même genre de travail qu'on peut surmonter ces difficultés.

Notes

1.Voir A. Brian McKillop, *A Disciplined Intelligence.* (Montreal: McGill-Queen's, 1979), p.1-21.

2.Plusieurs ne le considèrent pas comme philosophe. Voyez Thomas Goudge, compte rendu de *Philosophy in the Mass Age, University of Toronto Quarterly*, vol. 29 (JL 1960), p.486&7.

3.Voir McKillop p. 206-228, Leslie Armour & Elizabeth Trott, *The Faces of Reason* (Waterloo, Ont.: Wilfrid Laurier University Press, 1981), p.269-360.

4.Pour un commentaire très négatif mais néanmoins réaliste de l'impact culturel de la philosophie, voyez l'extrait de la lettre de O.D. Skelton à Adam Shortt, chez Brian Palmer, *A Culture in Conflict* (Montreal: McGill-Queen's, 1979), p. 236.

5.Claude Lévi-Strauss en est un bon exemple. Cfr. *Tristes Tropiques* (London: Atheneum, 1971), p.54-64.

6.Voir John M. MacEachran, "John Watson 1847-1934" in *Some Great Men of Queen's*, ed. par R.C. Wallace (Toronto: Ryerson, 1940), p.22-50.

7.Nous avons demandé à tous nos chercheurs de se poser une dernière question avant de rayer une notice en raison de manque de rapport, "Si ce n'est pas de la philosophie, qu'est-ce que c'est?".

8.Ainsi, même la polémique anti-catholique de John Strachan, telle que *Poor Man's Preservative Against Popery* (Toronto: Bull, 1834) et les traités d'éducation de Egerton Ryerson sont inclus dans la bibliographie en tant qu'exemples du travail intellectuel du début de l'histoire du Canada- anglais.

9.Albert-Marie Landry, "La pensée philosophique médiévale. Contribution canadienne (1960-1973)," *Philosophiques*, vol. 1 (OC1974), p111-39.

10.Il collabora également au *Canadian Monthly and National Review.* Voir McKillop, p. 157, 261.

11.Plusieurs des instruments et des techniques mentionnés s'avèrent également utiles en ce qui concerne d'autres travaux bio-bibliographiques.

12.De plus, le *Directory* comprend des revues, éditeurs et sociétés philosophiques canadiennes et américaines.

13.Armour et Trott mentionnent qu'au moment de la nomination de G.S. Brett, le département de philosophie de l'University of Toronto comptait sept membres et formait le département le plus important au Canada. (*The Faces of Reason*, p. 433). On note, cependant, que parmi ce nombre cinq membres s'occupaient principalement de la psychologie.

14. Certains auteurs dont les intérèts ou les audiences sont très specialisés demandent du travail supplementaire. Les indexes qui leur sont particulierement appropriés devront être consultés. Par exemple, la rédaction de la bibliographie d'Emil Fackenheim nécessita le dépouillement par Mark Rabnett des indexes de *Commentary, Conservative Judaism ainsi que l'Index of Articles on Jewish Studies, l'International Bibliography of Jewish Affairs*, et *l'Index to Jewish Periodicals.*

15. Une autre source est l'heureuse decouverte de collections de tirés à part dans les archives. Une telle collection concernant H.L. Stewart se retrouve aux archives de l'Université Dalhousie.

16. Quelquefois, cependant, la *Bibliography of Philosophy, Psychology and Cognate Subjects* de Benjamin Rand (New York: Macmillan, 1905, 2 vols.) qui a paru aussi comme vol. 3, pt. 1 & 2 de *Baldwin's Dictionary of Philosophy and Psychology* (N.Y.: Macmillan, 1905) peut se montrer utile. Par exemple, l'article sur la psychologie de l'enfant de James Mark Baldwin, rédigé lors de son séjour à Toronto se trouvent à proximité d'articles sur le même sujet publiés un peu plus tard par Frederick Tracy du même département. Un rechercheur qui s'intéresserait à l'influence de la philosophie sur le développement de la psychologie pourrait trouver cette information utile.

17. Voir Yvan Lamonde, *La philosophie et son enseignement au Québec (1665-1920)* (Ville LaSalle: Hurtubise HMH, 1980) p. 275-280 pour une liste.

18. En plus des archives de l'Université Dalhousie, les archives et les fonds de livres rares de l'Université de Toronto (y compris celles des collèges fédérés), de Queen's, McGill et Manitoba devraient s'avérer utiles à l'historien d'activités philosophiques. Au Québec, on devra porter attention aux archives à Laval et à l'Université de Montréal. Et l'Université d'Ottawa ainsi que les collèges classiques ne devraient pas être ignorés.

Part II

Secondary Sources

I make no claim that the list of bibliographies and historical pieces to follow is complete. It does not include, for example, numerous obituaries and memorial studies about deceased philosophers. It also does not include references to all of the items written about the institutional state of philosophy in Quebec, which are referred to in the bibliography of such material by Maurice Descoteaux, Dominique Gagné and Claude Savary. It does, however, contain a complete entry for that bibliography. It is hoped that what has been provided is a useful guide for researchers in the field. On the list 'c.r.' designates book reviews.

Deuxième Partie

Sources secondaires

Nous ne prétendons pas que la liste de bibliographies et de travaux historiques qui suit est complète. Elle ne comprend pas, par exemple, plusieurs notices nécrologiques et plusieurs études commémoratives. Elle ne comprend pas non plus, à la différence de la bibliographie de Maurice Descoteaux, Dominique Gagné et Claude Savary, des références à tous les écrits où il est question de l'état institutionnel de la philosophie au Québec. Elle comprend, par contre, une notice complète qui renvoie à cette bibliographie. On espère que ce qu'on a inclu s'avérera utile à ceux qui souhaitent effectuer des recherches dans le domaine de la philosophie. Dans la liste, 'c.r.' indique des contes rendus

.

1 W.J. Alexander, ed., *The University of Toronto and its colleges, 1827-1906.* Toronto: University of Toronto Press, 1906. 330p. Includes a list of publications of University staff members to 1906, p.230-56.

2 Bernard Amtmann, *Religion and philosophy in Canada.* Montreal: Bernard Amtmann Inc., 1961. (Catalogue 145). Catalogue of Canadiana in the fields of religion in philosophy, with bookstore list prices and some library locations.

3 Pierre Angers, *Philosophie et enseignement de philosophie.* Québec: Université Laval, 1969. 68p. Actes du 6e. semaine interuniversitaire de philosophie, Montréal, 29 & 30 mars 1969.

4 Leslie Armour, *Canadian philosophy and the national consciousness.* Paper delivered to the Conference on Canadian philosophy, Ottawa, 9MR1979. 24p. Available, B.P.C. office, Department of Philosophy, University of Toronto.

5 Leslie Armour, "Canadian philosophy: the nature and history of a discipline? A reply to Mr. Mathien." *Dialogue* 25/1 Spring 1986 67-82. A reply to no. 283.

6 Leslie Armour, "Charles De Koninck, the common good, and the human environment." *Laval Théologique et Philosophique* 43/1 FE1987 67-80. Résumé en français, p.67. On De Koninck's *De la primauté du bien commun contre les personnalistes*, and its foundations in De Koninck's philosophy of nature.

7 Leslie Armour, "Denominationalism and religion in Ontario." *Journal of Canadian Studies* 20/1 Spring 1985 25-38.

8 Leslie Armour, *The faces of reason. An essay on philosophy and culture in English Canada, 1850-1950.* By Leslie Armour and Elizabeth Trott. Waterloo: Wilfrid Laurier University Press, 1981. xxvi, 548p. Bibliographic footnotes. Author and titles indices p.517- 29. This extensive general history offers both discussion of the socio-cultural context of English Canadian thought in the period and extensive analyses of philosophic doctrines of the authors covered. There is special focus on idealistic views of reason as a means of overcoming social and ideological differences. Book reviews cited in no. 389.

9 Leslie Armour, *The idea of Canada and the crisis of community.* Ottawa: Steel Rail Publishing, 1982. 180p. Annotated bibliography, p.171-80. Illustrations. This discussion of Canadian nationality, and various "ideas and images of it" contains an extensive treatment of philosophic reflections on the topic, notably in Part 2. Chapter 8 comprises a later version of no. 4.

10 Leslie Armour, *The industrial kingdom of God*. By John Clark Murray, Ed. from manuscripts by Leslie Armour & Elizabeth Trott, with prefatory material by the editors. Ottawa: University of Ottawa Press, 1982. xxx, 144p. The bibliographical sketch of Murray (p.xi-xiii) and the preface which sets his thought in the context of economic thinking in 19th century Canada (p.xv-xxix) are of interest.

11   Leslie Armour, "Religion et philosophie au Québec et au Canada anglais." *Philosophiques* 11/2 OC1982 307-16. Intervention sur *La philosophie et son enseignement au Québec*, par Yvan Lamonde (no. 220)

12   Leslie Armour, "The social and philosophical origins of rational religion in Quebec and English Canada." *Friendship and dialogue between Ontario and Quebec*. Ed. Henri-Paul Cunningham & F. Temple Kingston. Windsor: Canterbury College, University of Windsor, 1985.

13 Brother Azarias, "Philosophy at the University of Alberta." *Culture* 2/4 DC1941, 508-12. One of a series of articles on philosophy in Canadian universities published in *Culture* in 1941.

14   Alfred Goldsworthy Bailey, *Culture and nationality*. Toronto: McClelland and Stewart, 1972. 224p. A discussion of 19th Century English-Canadian political culture and of reactions during the period to literary movements and evolutionary theory.

15   Hermas Bastien, *Ces écrivains qui nous habitent*. Montréal: Beauchemin, 1969. Bibliographie de l'auteur p.193-227.

16   Hermas Bastien, *L'enseignement de la philosophie* I, *Au Canada français*. Montréal: Editions Albert Lévesque, 1936. 222p.

17   Jacques Beaudry, *Autour de Jacques Lavigne, philosophe*. Trois-Rivières: Editions du Bien Public, 1985. 168p. Bibliographie: Textes de Jacques Lavigne 159-61; Autres textes à consulter, 161-3. Choix du textes de Lavigne, 57-158. Cet ouvrage présent la vie et les oeuvres de l'auteur de *L'inquietude humaine*.

18 Jacques Beaudry, *Bio-bibliographie de Roland Houde*. Trois-Rivières: Editions Fragments, 1983. 53p. ("Les Cahiers gris," 1). Essai de bibliographie et présentation d'inédits avec chronologie 1935-83.

19   Jacques Beaudry, *Philosophie et périodiques québécois: répertoire préliminaire* 1902-82. Trois-Rivières: Editions Fragments, 1983. 131p. ("Les Cahiers gris," 2).

20   Jacques Beaudry, *Roland Houde, un philosophe et sa circonstance*. Trois-Rivières: Editions du Bien Public, 1986. 195p. Bibliographie: Textes de Roland Houde, p.171-81; Autres textes à consulter, p.181-5. Essai biographique avec une sélection du textes de Roland Houde.

21   Paul Beaulieu, "Alexis Klimov, poète-philosophe," *Ecrits du Canada-Français* 53 1984 205-8.

22   Paul Beaulieu, "Choix des lettres: Jacques et Raïssa Maritain à Paul Beaulieu, Robert Charbonneau, Jean LeMoyne, Guy Sylvestre," *Ecrits du Canada-Français* 49 1983 5-114.

23   Lucien Beauregard, "La part de M. Isaac-Stanislas Desaulniers à l'introduction du thomisme au Canada français vers l'époque de la renaissance religieuse de 1840 à 1855." *Société canadienne d'histoire de l'Eglise catholique*. Rapport 1941-42 77-88.

24   Thomas C. Bechtle, *Dissertations in philosophy accepted at American universities, 1861-1975*. By Thomas C. Bechtle and Mary F. Riley. New York & London: Garland Publishing Co., 1978. 537p. The listing includes dissertations prepared for Canadian universities and is numbered, alphabetized by author, and indexed.

25   Pierre Bellehumeur, "Les situations paralleles de la philosophie en Amérique latine et au Québec." *Phi Zéro* 5/2 MA1977 5-18. Discussion sur les variétés de la colonisation intellectuelle.

 26   Louise Bender, *Bibliographie de Mgr. Louis-Adolphe Paquet*. Thèse présentée à l'Ecole de bibliothécaire de l'Université de Montréal, 1943. vii, 320p.

27   Carl Berger, *Science, God and nature in Victorian Canada*. Toronto: University of Toronto Press, 1983. xiv, 92p. (Joanne Goodman lecture series, 1982). Bibliographical notes. Deals with the response of Canadian intellectuals, particularly those of orthodox religious conviction, to the theory of evolution and related 19th century scientific developments. c.r.: *Isis* 76/281 MR1985 129 (Frank M. Turner).

28   Carl Berger, *The sense of power*. Toronto: University of Toronto Press, 1976. 277p. Discusses the ideas of English Canadian imperialists and suggests that some relied on an underlying social philosophy.

29   Carl Berger, *The writing of Canadian history*. Toronto: University of Toronto Press, 1976. x,300p. Bibliographical notes. Useful for a discussion of various schools of history writing in Canada, for a treatment of Harold Innis, and for comments--often in notes--on the philosophic interests and training of a number of English Canadian Victorians, e.g., Adam

Shortt. 2ed., 1986. 364p. Chapter on contemporary Canadian historiography 259-320. Bibliographical note, 321-3. End notes 324-52.

30 Jean-Paul Bernard, *Les idéologies québécoises au xixe siècle.* Montréal: Boreal Express, 1973. 151p. (Etudes d'histoire du Québec, 5).

31   Pierre Bertrand, "L'enseignement de la philosophie au Cégep." *Phi Zéro* 10/1 DC1981 65-75.

32 "Bibliography of John Watson." *Philosophical essays presented to John Watson.* Kingston: Queen's University, 1922. 343-6.

33 "Bibliography of the writings of John Clark Murray between 1867 and 1894." *Proceedings of the Royal Society of Canada* 12 1894 61-2.

34   "Bibliography of Watson Kirkconnell." *Acadia Bulletin* 47/1 1961 19-23. Contains a few items of philosophical interest.

35   Claude T. Bissell, "Literary taste in central Canada during the late Nineteenth Century." *Canadian Historical Review* 31/3 1950 235-51. Especially useful for a discussion of *The Week.*

36 Julian Blackburn, "George Humphrey." *Canadian Journal of Psychology* 11/3 SE1957 141-50. Humphrey was professor of philosophy and psychology at Queen's and a major early figure in experimental psychology.

37 Michel Blais, "Logique au Québec," Discussion par Michel Blais, Yvon Gauthier & Serge Robert. *Dialogue* 18/3 1979 405-17.

38   Yvon Blanchard, "Situation de la philosophie au Canada français." *L'enseignement de la philosophie - Recherches et débats du Centre catholique des intellectuels français*, cahier 36 1961 197-201.

39   Robert Boily, *Québec 1940-1969, bibliographie: Le système politique québécois et son environment.* Préf. de Jean- Charles Bonenfant. Montréal: Presses de l'Université de Montréal, 1971.

40   Raoul Bonin, *Bibliographie sulpicienne.* Archives Saint- Sulpice de Montréal. Sur fiches.

41   Claude Bonnelly, "Bibliographie d'Emile Simard." *Laval Théologique et Philosophique* 25 1969 168-70.

42   D.H. Borchardt, *How to find out in philosophy and psychology.* New York: Pergamon Press, 1968. 95p. Includes bibliographies.

43 John George Bourinot, *Bibliography of the members of the Royal Society of Canada*, printed by order of the society May 25th, 1894. 79p. Bound in *Royal Society of Canada, Transactions* 12 1894.

44 Gilles Bourque, "Les classes sociales et idéologies nationalistes au Québec 1760-1970." *L'Homme et la Société* 24-25 AL-SE1972 45p. Abr. trans in *Capitalism and the national question in Canada*. Ed. Gary Teeple. Toronto: University of Toronto Press, 1972. 185-210.

45 Alan Franklin Bowkes, *Truly useful men: Maurice Hutton, George Wrong, James Mavor and the University of Toronto, 1880-1927*. Toronto: 1975. ix, 457 leaves. Bibliography: leaves 410-57. Ph.D. Dissertation, University of Toronto.

46 Jacques Brault, "Pour une philosophie québécoise." *Parti Pris* 2/7 MR1965 9-16.

47 David Braybrooke, "The philosophical scene in Canada." *Canadian Forum* 53/636 JA1974 29-34. Maintains that there is a concentration of philosophical work in Canada in ethics, social and political philosophy.

48 John Bartlett Brebner, *Scholarship for Canada: the function of graduate studies*. Ottawa: Canadian Social Science Research Council, 1945. 90p.

49 George Sydney Brett, "Philosophy teaching in the University of Toronto." *Culture* 2/4 1941 434-5. Gives average numbers of students in undergraduate and graduate study at Toronto.

50 Marcelle Brisson, "L'écriture réflexive au Québec." *La Nouvelle Barre du Jour* 60 NO1977 54-63.

51 Jean-Paul Brodeur, "De l'orthodoxie en philosophie. A propos de l'Academie canadienne Saint-Thomas d'Aquin." *Philosophiques* 3 OC1976 209-53. L'Académie a publiée une collection annuelle des articles présentés à ses réunions.

52 Jean-Paul Brodeur, "Quelques notes critiques sur la philosophie québécoise." *La philosophie et les savoirs*. Montréal: Bellarmin 1975. (Coll. "L'Univers de la Philosophie") 237-73.

53 Jean-Paul Brodeur, "Se taire, dit-il?" *Philosophiques* 6/1 AL1979 201-7. Réponse à la critique par Roland Houde, intitulée "A propos," de no.51. Cfr. no.154, 172.

54 John R. Burr, *Handbook of world philosophy, contemporary developments since 1945*. Westport, Conn.: Greenwood Press, 1980. Section on Canadian philosophy, p.329-349: General discussion, p.329-31, "Anglophone philosophy" by John King-Farlow and Calvin G. Normore, p.331-42, "Francophone philosophy" by Jean-Paul Brodeur, p.342-9.

55 Robert E. Butts, "Philosophy of science in Canada." *Zeitschrift für Allgemeine Wissenschaftstheorie* 5/2 1974 341-58. Bibliographical.

56   Delano Dexter Calvin, *Queen's University at Kingston; the first century of a Scottish-Canadian foundation, 1841- 1941*. Kingston: Trustees of the University, 1941. xi, 321p. Bibliography p.309-12.

57   John Campbell, "The Reverend Professor James Beaven, D.D.,M.A." *University of Toronto Monthly* 3/3 DC1902 69-72. An early notice of the first professor of philosophy at the University of Toronto.

58   *The Canadian biographical dictionary, a portrait gallery of eminent and self-made men*. Toronto: American Biographical Publishing Co., 1881. 2 vols. vol 1- Ontario; vol 2-Quebec and the Maritime Provinces.

59   Pierre Cantin, *Bibliographie de la critique de la littérature québécoise dans les revues des XIXe et XXe siècles*. Par Pierre Cantin, Norman Harrington & Jean-Paul Hudson, Ottawa: Centre de Recherche en Civilisation Canadienne-française, 1979. (Documents de travail no. 12) Vol 1, p.134-5 recense matériaux sur Maurice Lebel, Jean Marcel, Robert Vigneault, Fernand Dorais.

60   Gaston Carrière, "Apôtres de la plume. Contributions des professeurs des facultés ecclésiatiques de l'Université d'Ottawa (1931-1951) à la bibliographie des Oblats de Marie-Immaculée." *Missions des Missionaires Oblats de Marie-Immaculée* 78 1951 140-52, 291-304.

61   Gaston Carrière, "Un authentique universitaire: le P. Roméo Trudel, o.m.i." *Revue de l'Université d'Ottawa* 24/4 1964 465-7.

62   Gaston Carrière, "Bibliographie des professeurs oblats des facultés ecclésiastiques de l'Université d'Ottawa (1932- 1961)." *Revue de l'Université d'Ottawa* 32/2 1962 81-104, 215-44. La liste comprend des ouvrages en philosophie & en théologie dogmatique ainsi bien que des ouvrages en théologie pastorale, liturgie, droit canonique et écriture sainte.

63   Gaston Carrière, *Cardinal Villeneuve: bibliographie*. Archive. Université d'Ottawa, s.d.

64   Gaston Carrière, "Le Collège de Bytown (1841-1861)." *Revue de l'Université d'Ottawa* 26 1956 56-78, 224-45, 317- 49.

65   Gaston Carrière, *L'Univerité d'Ottawa (1848-1861)*. Ottawa: Editions de l'Université, 1960. 96p.

66   John R. Catan, "Complete bibliography of Joseph Owens C.Ss.R." *Aristotle: the collected papers of Joseph Owens*. Edited by John R. Catan. Albany: State University of New York Press, 1981. 229-39. A thorough bibliography of primary sources, organised chronologically. Includes minor inaccuracies.

67 Venant Cauchy, "*Dialogue*, ou les bienfaits du pluralisme." *Dialogue* 25/1 Printemps 1986 7-10. Sur l'histoire et les buts du *Dialogue*.

68 Venant Cauchy, "Philosophy in French Canada: its past and future." *Dalhousie Review* 48/3 1968 384-401.

69 Venant Cauchy, "Principaux travaux philosophiques de Louis Lachance." *Dialogue* 2/4 1964 462-3.

70 Marc Chabot, *Figures de la philosophie québécoise après les troubles de 1837...* Montréal: Université du Québec à Montréal, Dépt. de philosophie, 1985. 525p. ("Recherches et Théories," 29). Avec bibliographies.

71 Marc Chabot, *Objets pour la philosophie*. Collectif dirigé par Marc Chabot & André Vidricaire. 2 vols. Vol. I *Nationnalisme, prostitution, syndicalisme, etc....* Québec: Les Editions Pantoute, 1983. 293p. (Collection Indiscipline). Vol. II *Création, desir, enseignement....* Québec: Les Editions Pantoute, 1985. 175p. (Collection Indiscipline). Présentations sur les objets propres à philosophie au Québec. c.r.: (Vol. I): *Philosophiques* 12/2 Aut1985 421-8 (Yvan Cloutier).

72 Marc Chabot, *La pensée québécoise de 1900 à 1950*. Bibliographie des textes parus dans les périodiques québécois. Trois-Rivières: Université de Québec à Trois- Rivières, 1975. 65p. Introduction p.i-v; Bibliographie 1-65.

73 François Charbonneau, *Les professeurs de philosophie des collèges du Québec*. Par F. Charbonneau, Normand Lacharité & André Vidricaire. Québec: Ministère de l'Education, Direction de l'Enseignement Collégial, 1972. (Rapport de l'Enquête APPE 1967-70) 4 vols., polycopies.

74 J.-P. Chalifoux, *Bio-bibliographies et bibliographies*. Québec: Bibliothèque Nationale, 1970. 60p.

75 Adrienne Choquette, *Confidences d'écrivains canadiens- français*. Ed. par Adrienne Choquette. Trois-Rivières: Editions du Bien Public, 1939. 237p. Etude de la culture intellectuelle de Québec jusqu'à 1939, relevée d'entretiens avec les auteurs de l'époque.

76 Hans George Classen, "The relevance of philosophy." *Queen's Quarterly* 84/1 Spring 1977 1-17. Includes comments from many philosophers on the state of the art in Canada.

77 H. McD. Clokie, "Canadian contributions to political science." *Culture* 3 1942 467-74.

78 Yvan Cloutier, "Des modes philosophiques: le cas Sartre." Polycopie, 13p., Tableaux. Sur la mode sartrienne à Québec de 1946 à 1950 et ses effets intellectuels dans les années 50 et 60.

79 Michel Collins, "L'historiographie comme jugement historique." *Phi Zéro* 3/2 MR1975 47-63. Critique du livre d'Yvan Lamonde: *Historiographie...*, no. 217.

80 Eugene Coombs, *Modernity and responsibility: essays for George Grant.* Ed. Eugene Coombs. Toronto: University of Toronto Press, 1983. xvii, 139p. Bibliography of George Grant (to 1982), p.133-8. c.r.: *Dialogue* 25/1 Spring 1986 191-3 (Wesley Cragg).

81 Ramsay Cook, *The regenerators: social criticism in late Victorian English Canada.* Toronto: University of Toronto Press, 1985. 291p. A discussion of the impact of secularism and criticism on Victorian thought. Includes discussions of certain philosophers.

82 Jacques Cotnam, *Contemporary Quebec: an analytical bibliography.* Toronto: McClelland & Stewart, 1973. 112p. Includes reference to works of philosophic relevance under headings such as "Culture", "Education", "Religion", etc.

83 Wesley Cragg, *Contemporary moral issues.* Toronto: McGraw-Hill Ryerson, 1983. A collection of readings on ethical issues composed entirely from Canadian sources. Includes bibliographic references on the topics covered. 2nd.: 1987 viii, 600p.

84 Wesley Cragg, "Two concepts of community, or moral theory and Canadian culture." *Dialogue* 25/1 Spring 1986 31-52. Contrasts George Grant's contribution to social theory in Canada with liberal positions in social philosophy.

85 Donald George Creighton, *Harold Adams Innis: portrait of a scholar.* Toronto: University of Toronto Press, 1957. 146p. Important biography of a scholar whose work crosses discipline boundaries and includes material of philosophic interest.

86 Frederick E. Crowe, "Bibliography of Bernard Lonergan." *Continuum* 2/3 Autumn 1964 544-9. Superseded by the more extensive but less readily available compilation of Tekippe and O'Callaghan, (no. 384). Contains references to some secondary sources.

87 André Dagenais, *Vingt-quatres défauts thomistes, Mémoire sur l'éducation.* Montréal: Editions du Lys, 1964. 206p.

88 Jaromir Danek, *Verité et ethos: recueil commemoratif dedié à Alphonse-Marie Parent.* Québec: Presses de l'Université Laval, 1982, xxxvi, 405p. c.r.: *Dialogue* 22/3 SE1983 (Pierre Bellemare).

89 Ioan Davies, *Philosophy in Canada: a report to the Canadian Philosophical Association on the philosophical survey 1969-71.* Kingston: Queen's University, Department of Sociology, 1972. 24p., tables. Copy available in office of the Bibliography of Philosophy in Canada. cf. no. 408.

90 Vianney Décarie, "La philosophie à l'université." *Cité Libre* JN-JL 1964 27-9.

91 Vianney Décarie, "La recherche en philosophie au Canada française." *La recherche au Canada française.* Montréal: Presses de l'Université de Montréal pour la Société Royale du Canada, 1968. 143-8.

92 Richard T. DeGeorge, *The philosophers guide to sources, research tools, professional life, and related fields.* Lawrence, Kansas: Regent's Press of Kansas, 1980. x, 261p. A very good general guide to the discipline and its bibliography. Includes discussion of a wide variety of research tools and techniques. Contains some references to Canadian material.

93 Charles De Koninck, "La philosophie au Canada de langue française." *Royal Commission studies. A selection of essays prepared for the Royal Commission on National Development in the Arts, Letters and Sciences.* Ottawa: King's Printer, 1951, 135-43. Repr. *Laval Théologique et Philosophique* 8 1952 103-11.

94 Frédéric Deloffre, "Du vrai sauvage à bon sauvage; La Hontan, Robert Challe et 'La Grand Gueule'." *Revue De l'Université D'Ottawa* 56/1 JA-MR1986 67-79.

95 Maurice Descoteaux, "La situation institutionelle de la philosophie universitaire au Québec." Pres. par Maurice Descoteaux, Dominique Gagné & Claude Savary. *Matériaux pour l'histoire des institutions universitaires de philosophie au Québec.* Vol. 2. Québec: Université Laval. Institut superieur des Sciences Humaines, 1976. (Cahiers de l'ISSH no. 4, t.2) Présentation p.134, Bibliographie p. 135-153. Bibliographie des écrits sur l'histoire des institutions universitaires de l'activité philosophique au Québec.

96 Gilles Dolbec, "Le premier docteur en science médiévales de l'Université de Toronto." *Revue Dominicaine* 54/1 1948 178-80. Entrevue avec Benoît Lacroix touchant les activités de P.I.M.S. jusqu'à 1948.

97 Leo Dorais, *L'autogestion universitaire: autopsie d'un mythe.* Montréal: Presses de l'Université du Québec, 1977. 130p. Comprend des bibliographies. Analyse de l'expérience du Departement de philosophie à l'Université du Québec à Montréal.

98   François Duchesneau, "Une étape dans l'histoire de *Dialogue*." *Dialogue* 25/1 Printemps 1986 5-6. Introduction, par le rédacteur francophone, au numéro de la 25e anniversaire. Duchesneau discute l'absence des contributions francophone sur "philosophie au Canada" dans ce numéro.

99   Fernand Dumont, "Une contribution à l'histoire de la philosophie au Québec." *Philosophiques* 10/1 AL1983 119- 25. A propos de Lamonde, *La philosophie et son enseignement...*no. 220.

100   Fernand Dumont, *Les idéologies au Canada-français (1900- 1929)*. Ed. par Fernand Dumont, Jean Hamelin, Fernand Harvey & J.-P. Montminy. Québec: Presses de l'Université Laval, 1974.   (Histoire et sociologie de la culture no. 6) 377p.

101   Fernand Dumont, "Idéologies au Canada-français, 1850- 1900-- quelques réflexions d'ensemble." *Recherches Sociographiques* 10/2-3 1969 145-6.

102   Callistus James Edie, "The writings of Etienne Gilson, chronologically arranged." *Mélanges offerts à Etienne Gilson de l'Académie Française*. Toronto: Pontifical Institute of Mediaeval Studies, 1959. A primary source bibliography; includes analytic notations not all of which are reproduced by Margaret McGrath, no. 257.

103 H. Martyn Estall, "*Dialogue*: 1961-1986." *Dialogue* 25/1 Spring 1986 11-15. An historical note on the beginnings of *Dialogue*.

104   *Ethics, value and reality*. Selected papers of Aurel Thomas Kolnai. Compiled by Francis Dunlop and Brian Klug. Biography by David Wiggins and B.A.O. Williams   Bibliography compiled with the aid of Elizabeth Kolnai. London: University of London - The Athlone Press, 1977. Biography p.ix-xxv. Bibliography p.226-37. Hungarian by birth, Austrian in education, Kolnai, an anti-fascist of Jewish descent, spent the 1940's and part of the 1950's in Canada at Laval. He later taught at the University of London.

105   Mostafa Faghfoury, *Analytical philosophy of religion in Canada*. Ed. by Mostafa Faghfoury. Ottawa: University of Ottawa Press, 1982. xiv. 288p. Includes texts by and commentaries on Terrence Penelhum, Kai Nielsen, Alastair McKinnon and Donald Evans. c.r.: *Dialogue* 22/4 DC1983 750-4 (James R. Horne).

106 Nadia Fahmy-Eid, *L'idéologie ultramontaine au Québec (1848-1871): composantes, manifestations et signification au niveau de l'histoire sociale de la période.* Montréal: 1974. Thèse (Ph.D. Histoire) Université de Montréal. vii. 421p.

107 Nadia Fahmy-Eid, "Ultramontanisme, idéologie et classes sociales." *Revue d'histoire de l'Amérique Française* 29 JN1975 49-68.

108 Jean-Charles Falardeau, *Etienne Parent 1802- 1874/Biographie,textes et bibliographie.* Présentés par J.-C. Falardeau. Montréal: La Presse, 1975. 344p. (Collection Echanges) Bibliographie p.327-36. Parent fut publiciste pour les causes libérales au Québec durant le 19e siècle.

109 Albert Fiorino, "The moral education of Egerton Ryerson's idea of education." *Egerton Ryerson and his times.* Ed. Neil McDonald & Alf Chaiton. Toronto: Macmillan of Canada, 1978. 59-80. Connects Ryerson's educational policy with his moral theories which were appropriated from Methodist sources and from Paley and which display a tension between them.

110 Albert Fiorino, *The philosophical roots of Egerton Ryerson's idea of education as elaborated in his writings preceding and including the report of 1846.* Toronto: 1975. Ph.D. Dissertation. 253 leaves. Bibliography l.247-53.

111 Frank K. Flinn, "George Parkin Grant: a bibliographical introduction." and "A bibliography of George Parkin Grant." *George Grant in process. Essays and conversation.* Ed. by Larry Schmidt. Toronto: Anansi, 1978. p.195-9, 200-3. An excellent primary bibliography of Grant.

112 Marie-Ceslas Forest, "Rôle d'une faculté de philosophie dans une université moderne." *Culture* 2/4 1941 419-21. Avec commentaires de l'auteur sur le rôle qu'il envisage pour la philosophie et sur son institution-nalisation à l'Université de Montréal.

113 Marcel Fournier, "L'institutionnalisation des sciences sociales au Québec." *Sociologie et sociétés* 5/1 MA1973 27-59. Avec considérations sur la rapport entre les sciences sociales et la discipline de la philosophie au Québec.

114 Marcel Fournier, "Les conflits de discipline: philosophie et sciences sociales au Québec 1920-1960." *Philosophie au Québec.* Ed. par Claude Panaccio et P.-A. Quintin. Montréal: Bellarmin, 1976. (L'Univers de la Philosophie, no. 5) 207-36.

115 Stanley G. French, "Considérations sur l'histoire et l'esprit de la philosophie au Canada-français." *Cité Libre* JN-JL1964 20-6. Contient une interpretation importante mais contestable de l'histoire de la philosophie au Québec.

116   Stanley G. French, *Philosophers look at Canadian confederation/La confédération canadienne: qu'en pensent les philosophes?*. Montréal: Canadian Philosophical Association/L'Association Canadienne de Philosophie, 1979. 407p. Avec une bibliographie sur la question nationale, présentés par Myrna Friend, p.389-407.

117   Gernot U. Gabel, *Canadian theses on German philosophy 1925-1975: A bibliography*. 2ed. rev. Köln: Gemini, 1984. 47p. (Bibliographien zur philosophie, Bd.6).

118   Armand Gagné, "Bibliographie de Charles de Koninck." *Itinéraires* 66 1962 141-59.

119   Armand Gagné, "Bibliographie de Charles de Koninck de 1933 à 1965." *Mélanges à la mémoire de Charles de Koninck.* Québec: Presses Universitaires de Laval, 1968. 9-22. De Koninck fut un personnage prééminent en philosophie au Québec et chez les philosophes catholiques Nord Amérique.

120   Claude Gagnon, "Répertoire des thèses de doctorat en philosophie contenues dans les universités au Québec des origines à 1978," par Claude Gagnon & Denise Pelletier. *Bulletin de la Société de Philosophie du Québec.* 5 1979.

121   Claude Galarneau, *Les collèges classiques au Canada français (1620-1970)*. Montréal: Fides, 1978. 287p. Les collèges classiques fournirent le lieu principal pour l'enseignement de la philosophie avant la révolution tranquille.

122   Claude Galarneau, "L'enseignement des sciences au Québec et Jérôme Demers (1765-1835)." *Revue de l'Université d'Ottawa* 47/1-2 JA-AL1977 84-94.

123   Donald A. Gallagher, *The achievement of Jacques and Raïssa Maritain. A bibliography 1906-1961*, by Donald Gallagher and Idella Gallagher. Garden City, New York: Doubleday, 1962. Maritain had considerable influence in Quebec and in Catholic institutions in English Canada.

124   Benôit Garceau, "La philosophie analytique de la religion: contribution canadienne 1970-1975." *Philosophiques* 2/2 OC1975 301-39.

125   Edmond Gaudron, "French Canadian philosophers." *Culture of Contemporary Canada.* Ed. by Julian Park. Ithaca, New York: Cornell University Press, 1957. 274-92.

126   Edmond Gaudron, "La philosophie et les universités canadiennes." *Culture* 2/4 1941 477-91.

127   Georges-Hébert Germain, "Les pourquoi d'un philosophe," *L'Actualité* 11/6 JN1986 13-7. Entretien avec Charles Taylor.

128 Nicole Godin, "Colloque de la jeune philosophie," par Nicole Godin, Jocelyne Simard, Marcelle Brisson & Serge Therien. *Phi Zéro* 8/2 JN1980 67-119.   Le deuxième atelier du colloque (tenu 14-16 MR1980 à l'Université du Québec à Montréal) traite de la philosophie québécoise.

129   Crawford D.W. Goodwin, *Canadian economic thought: the political economy of a developing nation, 1814-1914*. Durham, N.C.: Duke University Press for the Duke University Commonwealth Studies Center, 1961. xvi, 214p. Bibliographical footnotes. Deals with a period when political economy was still closely linked with philosophy and frequently carried normative elements.

130   Paul-Eugène Gosselin, *Etienne Parent, 1802-1874. Textes choisis et présentés par Paul-Eugène Gosselin.* Montréal: Fides, 1964. (Collections Classiques Canadiens, 27) 95p. Avec bibliographie.

131   Thomas A. Goudge, "A century of philosophy in English- speaking Canada." *Dalhousie Review* 47/4 1968 537-49. An important discussion of the history of philosophy in English Canada to 1967.

132   Thomas A. Goudge, "Complex disguises: reason in Canadian philosophy." *Dialogue* 22/2 JN1983 339-46. Critical notice of Leslie Armour & Elizabeth Trott, *The faces of reason* (no. 8). The article comments critically on the notions of reason, culture and Canadian philosophy employed in the book.

133   Thomas A. Goudge, *Instruction and research in philosophy at the University of Toronto. A historical sketch of the development of philosophy.* By Thomas A. Goudge and John G. Slater. Toronto: Department of Philosophy, University of Toronto, 1977. 42p. A detailed history of one of the major philosophy departments in Canada--one of the largest English-speaking philosophy departments in the world.   Part I 1827-1969 by Thomas A. Goudge; Part II 1969-1974 by John G. Slater.

134   Thomas A. Goudge, "Philosophical literature: 1910-1960." *Literary history of Canada*, rev. ed. vol. 2. Ed. by Carl Klinck. Toronto: University of Toronto Press, 1976. 95- 107. With bibliographic references. Replaces Irving and Johnson articles in original Klinck volume, no. 197.

135   Thomas A. Goudge, "Philosophical literature: 1960-1973." *Literary history of Canada*, rev. ed. vol. 3. Ed. by Carl Klinck. Toronto: University of Toronto Press, 1976. 84- 103. With bibliographic references. Covers a period not discussed in the earlier edition of Klinck's *Literary history*...

136   George Parkin Grant, "The academic study of religion in Canada." *Scholarship in Canada, 1967: achievement and outlook:* symposium presented to the Royal Society of Canada in 1967. Ed. by R.H. Hubbard. Toronto: University of Toronto Press, 1967. 59-68. Grant has been an influential philosopher, religious thinker and social theorist. His survey items will reflect his general views about Canada.

137   George Parkin Grant, "Philosophy." *Encyclopedia Canadiana*, vol. 8. Toronto: Grolier, 1957. 183-4.

138   George Parkin Grant, "Philosophy." *Royal commission studies: a selection of essays prepared for the Royal Commission on National Development in the Arts, Letters and Sciences.* Ottawa: King's Printer, 1951. 111-34.

139   William Gray, *Unity through diversity: a Festschrift in honour of Ludwig von Bertalanffy.* New York: Gordon and Breach, 1973. 2 vols. xxii. 1141p. (Current Topics of Contemporary Thought, vol. 9). Includes a bibliography of about 280 entries, consisting of von Bertalanffy's works. Bertalanffy, a biologist and founder of general systems theory, spent a substantial part of his post-World War II career in Canada.

140   A.H. Greenly, "Lahontan: an essay and bibliography." *Papers of the Bibliographical Society of America* 48 1954 334-89. Also issued as an offprint, 89p. Baron Lom d'Arce de Lahontan spent ten years in New France and produced a discussion of his travels together with an invented dialogue with a Huron chief on matters of human nature, custom and religion. This dialogue had considerable influence on thinkers of the French enlightenment.

141   Groupe du travail, Conseil des Universités du Québec, *Dossier philosophie.* Québec: L'éditeur officiel du Québec, 1974. 62p. et commentaires. Avec discussion de l'histoire et de l'état actuel de la philosophie au Québec.

142   Herbert Guerry, *A bibliography of philosophical bibliographies.* Westport, Conn.: Greenwood Press, 1977. Lists bibliographies by individual philosopher covered, and by subject.

143   Armand Guilmette, "*Eloge de l'homme inutile* d'Alexis Klimov et hommage à Alexis Klimov." *Lettres Québécoises* 36 Hiver 1984-5 84.

144   Alois Gutzwiller, *Guide du choix des livres en philosophie pour bibliothèques des collèges.* Préf. par Emile Simard. Montréal: Fédération des Collèges Classiques, 1966. xii, 372p. (Collection Livres et Bibliothèques--L.B. 801). Thèse, M.A.--Catholic University of America.

145 Willet Ricketson Haight, *Canadian catalogue of books, 1791-1897.* London: H. Pordes, 1958. 130, 49, 58p. Reprints Haight's catalogue 1791-1895 and the 1896 and 1897 supplements. An extensive but not exhaustive list of books issued by Canadian publishers.

146 Russell Hann, "Brain workers and the Knights of Labour: E.E. Sheppard, Phillips Thompson, and the *Toronto News*, 1883-1887." *Essays in Canadian working class history.* Ed. by Gregory S. Kealey & Peter Warrian. Toronto: McClelland and Stewart, 1976. 35-57. Discusses the role of the intellectual worker in industrial society and describes, as an example, the work of Phillips Thompson for Sheppard and the *News.* Thompson was an anti- establishment writer some of whose works touch philosophic topics.

147 Robin Harris, *A history of higher education in Canada, 1663-1960.* Toronto: University of Toronto Press, 1976. Bibliography, p.633-88; note section on philosophy, p.656- 7. Includes comments on the teaching of philosophy in humanities curricula during various periods of Canadian history and discussions of research and advanced degrees.

148 Michael Hayden, *Seeking a balance: the University of Saskatchewan, 1907-1982.* Vancouver: University of British Columbia Press, 1983. Includes extensive discussion of the role of Walter Murray, philosopher and first president of the university and lists of early appointments in philosophy and other disciplines.

149 Robert Hébert,"Contre la politique (généralisée) du réflexe pastoral, ou d'un problème en philosophie québécoise." *Revue et Corrigée* I/7-8 1982 17-27.

150 Robert Hébert, "D'une falaise d'où l'on voit poindre le soleil de la culture savante." Ptie. 1 *Philosophiques* 9/2 OC1982 281-93. Ptie. 2 *Philosophiques* 10/1 AL1983 97-110. Avec notes bibliographiques.

151 Robert Hébert, "Pensée québécoise et plaisir de la différence." *Brèches* 3 1974 31-9.

152 Charles William Hendel, "The character of philosophy in Canada." *University of Toronto Quarterly* 20/2 JA1951 124- 36. Also in *Philosophy and Phenomenological Research* 12/3 MR1952 365-76; *Philosophy in Canada*, Ed. John Irving. 27- 39.

153 F.W. Hill, "Philosophy at the University of British Columbia." *Culture* 2/4 DC1941 494-6.

154   Roland Houde, "A propos." *Phi Zéro* 6/2 MR1978 123-6. Sur J.-P. Brodeur "De l'orthodoxie en philosophie." (no. 51). Discussion historique de la rôle du thomisme au Québec.

155   Roland Houde, *Bibliographie de philosophie canadienne, 1867-1967.* Par Roland Houde et al. Sans éditeur. 7,491p. Liste des ouvrages publiés au Canada ou par Canadiens. Authors listed are identified by surname and first initial only. Exemplaire dans le bureau de la Bibliographie de la Philosophie au Canada.

156   Roland Houde, "Biblio-Tableau." *Philosophie au Québec.* Ed. Claude Panaccio & Paul-André Quintin. Montréal: Bellarmin, 1976. 179-205. Sur les influences intellectuelles dans la vie et l'oeuvre de Paul-Emile Borduas. Exemplaire de la méthode de recherche d'Houde et de sa polémique.

157   Roland Houde, *Carnapacité.* Trois-Rivières: 1982. 68p. ms. Texte, avec matériaux documentaires, d'une conférence présentée au congrès de A.C.P., 8JN1982; réaction critique à no. 316.

158   Roland Houde, "Errements ou incohérences." *Bulletin de la Societé de Philosophie du Québec* 2/2 FE1976 50. Autour d'une pseudo-référence à un texte de J.-P. Desbiens, dans l'*Histiographie...*(1972) de Y. Lamonde, no. 217.

159   Roland Houde, "Evolution des mentalités--de la plume/des modéles--Alexis Mailloux (1801-1877)." *Figures de la philosophie québécoise après les troubles de 1837.* Ed. par Marc Chabot. Montréal: Université du Québec à Montréal, Dépt. de philosophie, 1985, 229-78. ("Recherches at theories" 29).

160   Roland Houde, "Evolution du corps professoral (religieux et laïc) à Institut d'Etudes Médiévales de l'Université de Montréal--1942-74." *Fragments* 13 DC1983 1-4. Présentation par tables.

161   Roland Houde, "Fantaisies: de textes et de hommes, 1940- 1975." *Phi Zéro* 4/1 1975 41-60. Description de la situation nationale du livre au Québec. Projet d'édition d'une collection philosophique au Québec. Bibliographies.

162   Roland Houde, *Histoire et philosophie au Québec: Anarchéologie du savoir historique.* Trois-Rivières: Editions du Bien Public, 1979. 183p. Avec discussion d'histoires typiques de la philosophie. Contient extraits d'auteurs sur la philosophie au Québec. Notes bibliographiques. c.r.: *L'Information Médicale et Paramédicale* 29/17 19JL1977 20 (J.-P.

Légaré); *Livres et auteurs québécois* 1979 304-6 (Louise Marcil-Lacoste); *Philosophiques* 7/1 AL1980 93-100 (Robert Hébert).

163 Roland Houde, "Information, construction, critique; projections-- receptions." *Critère* 41 Printemps 1986 77-94.

164 Roland Houde, "Jacques et Raïssa Maritain au Québec II - éléments de bibliographie critique." *Relations* 384 JL- AU1973 214-7.

165 Roland Houde, "Mort dans la bibliothèque." *Dialogue* 12/3 1973 521-6. Repr. *Histoire et philosophie...* (no. 135) p.73-9. Intervention sur Yvan Lamonde, *Historiographie de la philosophie au Québec* (no. 217).

166 Roland Houde, "L'oeuvre philosophique de Charles de Koninck, bibliographie choisie et annotée." *Dialogue* 4/1 JN1965 99-101.

167 Roland Houde, "Pluralisme (philosophique et social) au Canada-- notes préliminaires et étapes historiques." *Fragments* 11-12 OC-NO1983 1-7.

168 Roland Houde, *Pour l'histoire de la philosophie au Québec, ou, anarchéologie du savoir philosophique, ou, réflexions méthodologiques pour une histoire de la philosophie québécoise.* Montréal: Société de la Philosophie de Montréal, 1976. 69p. miméographie.

169 Roland Houde, "Pour saluer Alexis Klimov--Reconnaissance de Marcel Raymond (1915-72)." *De la philosophie comme passion de la liberté- -Hommage à Alexis Klimov.* Québec: Beffroi, 1984. 171-5.

170 Roland Houde, "Projet philosophique dans une formation fon- damentale." *Memoires soumis au Conseil supérieur de l'education sur la formation fondamentale et la qualité de l'education par l'entremise du syn- dicat des professeurs de l'Université du Québec à Trois-Rivières.* Trois- Rivières: Syndicat des Professeurs de l'U.Q.T.R., 1984. 53-5.

171 Roland Houde, "La région--le sacre." *Critère* 23 1978 123- 6. Sur la role de la régionnalisation dans le champ de la culture philosophique au Québec.

172 Roland Houde, "La référence n'est pas à l'index (St. Thomas aujourd'hui)." *Philosophiques* 6/2 OC1979 341-6. Précisions sur les "actes" de l'Académie canadien Saint- Thomas d'Aquin et la relation entre celle-ci et la Société de la Philosophie de l'Université de l'Ottawa. cf. nos. 51, 53, 154.

173 Roland Houde, "Sartre ici--Bibliographie anatomique (préliminaire)." *La Petite Revue de Philosophie* 2/1 Aut1980 137-61.

174 Théophile Hudon, *L'institut canadien de Montréal et l'affaire Guibord: une page d'histoire.* Montréal: Beauchemin, 1938. 173p. Bibliographie p.171-2.

175 Institut d'Etudes Médiévales, Ottawa, "Une édition de saint Thomas au Canada." *Culture* 2 1941 129-53.

176 John Allan Irving, "The achievement of George Sydney Brett (1879-1944)." *University of Toronto Quarterly* 14 JL1945 329-65. Includes a check-list of Brett's work prepared by Katharine Wales, p.361-5. In several works, Irving has provided the first self-conscious treatment of the early development of philosophical studies in English Canada.

177 John Allan Irving, "The achievement of G.S. Brett." Adapted by Allison Heartz Johnson. *Literary history of Canada* 1 ed. Ed. Carl Klinck, Toronto: University of Toronto Press, 1965. 576-86. Comprises Part I of chapter 30, "Philosophical literature 1910-1964."

178 John Allan Irving, "The achievement of Thomas McCulloch." *The stepsure letters.* By Thomas McCulloch. Ed. Malcolm Ross. Toronto: McClelland and Stewart, 1960. (New Canadian Library, no. 16). 150-6. A brief biographical sketch of McCulloch, professor of philosophy at the Pictou Academy and first principal of Dalhousie College.

179 John Allan Irving, "The development of philosophy in central Canada from 1850 to 1900." *Canadian Historical Review* 31/3 SE1950 252-87.

180 John Allan Irving, "George Sydney Brett, 1879-1944." *Psychological Review* 54/1 JA1947 52-8.

181 John Allan Irving, "Philosophical trends in Canada between 1850 and 1950." *Philosophy and Phenomenological Research* 12/2 DC1951 224-45.

182 John Allan Irving, "Philosophy." *The culture of contemporary Canada.* Ed. Julian Park. Ithaca, New York: Cornell University Press, 1957. 242-73.

183 John Allan Irving, *Philosophy in Canada*, By John A. Irving et. al. Toronto: University of Toronto Press, 1952. 48p. Includes comments by Allison Heartz Johnson (p.40-3), Rupert C. Lodge (p.44-8) and Charles W. Hendel (p.27-39). Irving's contribution also appears under title "One hundred years of Canadian philosophy." *University of Toronto Quarterly.* 20/2 JA1951 107-23.

184 Mary Ann Jameson, *Richard Maurice Bucke. A catalogue based upon the collections of the University of Western Ontario Libraries.* Compiled by Daniel Brock, Mary Ann Jameson, Artem Lozynsky and Edward Phelps.

London, Ontario: University of Western Ontario, 1978. xvi, 126p. Bucke, a medical doctor and director of mental institutions in London and Hamilton, wrote a number of philosophically interesting works. This catalogue is not a complete primary bibliography; it reports only those items held at Western. However, it does include references to many editions of his major published works, to letters, to the holdings of his personal library and to secondary materials and other bibliographic resources.

185 Allison Heartz Johnson, "Comments I." *Philosophy in Canada, a symposium*. Ed. John Allan Irving. Toronto: University of Toronto Press, 1952. 40-3.

186 Allison Heartz Johnson, *The concept of Canadian philosophy*. Paper delivered to the conference on Canadian Philosophy, Ottawa. 9MR1979. 14p. Available, office of the Bibliography of Philosophy in Canada, Department of Philosophy, University of Toronto.

187 Allison Heartz Johnson, "Other philosophers." *Literary history of Canada*, 1 ed. Ed. Carl Klinck. Toronto: University of Toronto Press, 1965. 586-97. Comprises Part II of chapter 30, "Philosophical literature 1910-1964." A survey with selected bibliographical references.

188 Charles Murray Johnston, *McMaster University*. Toronto: University of Toronto Press, 1976-81. 2 vols.: vol. 1, *The Toronto years*, 1976; vol. 2, *The early years in Hamilton*, 1981. Bibliographic footnotes and notes on sources. Both volumes discuss the philosophy department. Vol. 1 includes discussion of James Ten Broeke.

189 George Johnston, *The church in the modern world; essays in honour of James Sutherland Thompson*. Ed. George Johnston and Wolfgang Roth. Toronto: Ryerson Press, 1976. Bibliography of James Sutherland Thompson p.306-7. Thompson is a major Protestant theologian with philosophical interests.

190 Ernest Joos, *The idea of Canadian philosophy*. Paper delivered to the Conference on Canadian Philosophy, Ottawa, 9MR1979. 9p. Avec préambule en français, p.1-2. Copy available in the office of the Bibliography of Philosophy in Canada.

191 "Joseph Owens CSSR: a bibliography." *Graceful reason: essays in ancient and medieval philosophy presented to Joseph Owens CSSR*. Ed. Lloyd P. Gerson. Toronto: Pontifical Institute of Mediaeval Studies, 1983. 419-33. Bibliography of Joseph Owens to mid-1982. Includes reference to reviews of Owens' books and critical articles about his work. Some cross-referencing.

192   Wilfred Currier Keirstead, "University of New Brunswick, past and present." *Dalhousie Review* 22/3 1943 344-54. A brief institutional history coupled with a discussion of the role that various subjects, including philosophy, should have in the curriculum.

193   John King-Farlow, "Philosophical nationalism: self- deception and self-direction." *Dialogue* 17/4 DC1978 591- 613. Discussion of the character of Canadian philosophy.

194   Watson Kirkconnell, *The humanities in Canada;* report of a survey of Canadian colleges and universities made by the Humanities Research Council of Canada. Drafted by W. Kirkconnell and A.S.P. Woodhouse in collaboration with other members of the council. Ottawa: Humanities Research Council, 1946. 2 vols.

195   Watson Kirkconnell, "Religion and philosophy: an English Canadian point of view." *Canadian Dualism*. Ed. Mason Wade. Toronto: University of Toronto Press, & Québec: Presses de l'Université Laval, 1960. 41-55.

196   Arthur G. Kirn, "Bibliography of the works--books, editions, articles, translations and reviews of Gerald B. Phelan." *Gerald B. Phelan: selected papers*. Ed. Arthur G. Kirn. Toronto: Pontifical Institute of Mediaeval Studies, 1967. 248p. Phelan was the first notable *scholar* in philosophy to be produced by the Basilian order in Canada, and was an early professor at the Pontifical Institute.

197   Carl Frederick Klinck, *Literary history of Canada; Canadian literature in English*, 1 ed. Ed. Carl Klinck. Toronto: University of Toronto Press, 1965. xiv, 945p. Bibliography and notes p.853-67. A general literary history of Canada which includes chapters on philosophic writing and on related subjects. One chapter on philosophy is replaced, not merely supplemented, in the latest edition. Tr: *Histoire littéraire du Canada; littérature canadienne de langue anglaise*. Tr. par Maurice Lebel. Québec: Presses de l'Université Laval, 1970. 1105p. Bibliographie p.1004-21.

198   Carl Frederick Klinck, *Literary history of Canada,* revised edition. Ed. Carl Klinck. Toronto: University of Toronto Press, 1976. 3 vols. In addition to articles on philosophy one should consult articles on related subjects: e.g., religion, social sciences, essay writing, etc.

199   Bonace O. Korchinski, *Evidence of the enlightenment in the Quebec newspapers (1785-1795)*. M.A. thesis (history) University of Saskatchewan, 1972. viii, 131p. Provides evidence of the earliest print references in Canada to philosophers and philosophic topics.

200 Henry J. Koren, *Research in philosophy*. Pittsburgh: Duquesne University Press & Louvain: Nauwelaerts, 1966. 203p. A good general guide; includes useful description of and instructions for the use of the *Répertoire bibliographique de la philosophie*.

201 Arthur Kroker, *Technology and the Canadian mind: Innis/McLuhan/Grant*. Montreal: New World Perspectives, 1984. 144p.

202 Pierre Laberge, "Dix années d'études canadokantiennes (1968-1978)." *Philosophiques* 5/2 OC1978 331-80. Bibliographie. Quelques articles renseignés datent d'avant 1968.

203 Normand Lacharité, "L'enseignement de la philosophie au Canada français de 1968 à 1970." *Revue de l'Enseignement Philosophique* 20/6 AU-SE1970 1-8.

204 Benoît Lacroix, "Les débuts de la philosophie universitaire à Montréal, les mémoires du doyen Ceslas Forest O.P. (1885-1970)." Par Yvan Lamonde & Benoît Lacroix. *Philosophiques* 3/1 AL1976 55-79.

205 Benoît Lacroix, "L'institut d'études médiévales." *L'Action Universitaire* 14JL1948 362-70. Avec notes bibliographiques.

206 Benoît Lacroix, "Pastorale en pré-histoire, un institut d'études médiévales." *Communauté Chrétienne* 12/70 JL- AU1973 285-96.

207 Benoît Lacroix, *Vie des lettres et histoire canadienne*. Montréal: Editions du Lévrier, 1954.

208 Yvon Lafrance, "Les études platoniciennes: contribution canadienne." *Philosophiques* 4/1 AL1977 51-99.

209 Maurice Lagueux, "A propos d'un livre sur la philosophie au Québec." *Dialogue* 12/3 1973 515-20. Re Yvan Lamonde, *Historiographie de la philosophie au Québec* (no. 217).

210 Maurice Lagueux, *Le marxisme des années soixante: une saison dans l'histoire de la pensée critique*. Ville LaSalle: Hurtubise HMH, 1982. (Collection Brèches). 350p. Bibliographie, p.323-33. Discussion de l'influence, au Québec, des developpements marxistes dans la pensée philosophique française et la théorie politico- économique américaine pendant les années 60. c.r.: *Revue Canadienne des Comptes Rendus en Philosophie* 3/2 72-7 (Roberto Miguelez).

211 Maurice Lagueux, "Réflexions sur l'enseignement de la philosophie au collègial." *Cité Libre* 12/56 AL1963 22-7. Réflexions sur les problèmes de la pédagogie philosophique en contexte québécois--pas une analyse sociologique de la situation.

212   Maurice Lagueux, "Simple réaction à un double commentaire." *Dialogue* 23/3 SE1984 493-501. Sur les commentaires par Christopher W. Morris (no. 294) et Claude Panaccio (no. 315) sur *Le marxisme des années soixante* (no. 210).

213   Yvan Lamonde, "Un almanach idéologique des années 1900- 1929: l'oeuvre de Mgr. L.-A. Paquet, théologien nationaliste." *Les idéologies au Canada-Français*. Québec: Presses de l'Université Laval, 1974. (Histoire et Sociologie de la Culture, no. 5) 251-65.

214   Yvan Lamonde, "L'enseignement de la philosophie au Collège de Montréal 1790-1876." *Culture* 31/2 JN1970 109-23; 31/3 SE1970 213-24; 31/4 DC1970 312-26.

215   Yvan Lamonde, "L'histoire de la philosophie au Canada- français (de 1920 à nos jours): sources et thèmes de recherche." *Philosophiques* 6/2 OC1979 324-39. Avec notes bibliographiques.

216   Yvan Lamonde, "Histoire et inventaire des archives de l'Institut canadien de Montréal." *Revue d'Histoire de l'Amérique Française* 28/1 JN1974 77-93. L'Institut était une association séculière pour l'éducation populaire et conférences publiques au milieu du 19e siècle, et un centre de pensée libérale sur questions socio-politiques au Québec.

217   Yvan Lamonde, *Historiographie de la philosophie au Québec, 1853-1970*. Préf. de Georges Leroux. Montréal: Hurtubise HMH, 1972. (Collection Philosophie - Les Cahiers du Québec) 245p. "Chronologie sommaire," 225-6. "Bibliographie chronologique," 227-36. Avec notes bibliographiques et reimpressions de commentaires sur la philosophie au Québec par L.-A. Pâquet, Arthur Robert, Hermas Bastien, et. al. cf. nos. 162, 165, 209. c.r.: *Recherches Sociographiques* 14/2 1973 270-1 (Pierre Thibault), *Revue d'Histoire de l'Amérique Française* 29/3 DC1975 435 (Marc Lebel).

218   Yvan Lamonde, *Louis-Adolphe Paquet*. Ed. par Yvan Lamonde. Montréal: Fides, 1972. (Classiques Canadiens). 86p. Collection de textes par Pâquet.

219   Yvan Lamonde, "Petite histoire de l'histoire de la philosophie au Canada-français." *Emergences* 2/1 SE-OC1967 3-7.

220   Yvan Lamonde, *La philosophie et son enseignement au Québec, (1665-1920)*. Ville LaSalle: Hurtubise, 1980. (Collection Philosophie--Les Cahiers du Québec). 312p. Bibliographie p.275-302. Avec notes bibliographiques. Une discussion nonpareille de l'institutionnalisation et rôle idéologique de la philosophie au Québec jusqu'à 1920. La bibliographie inclu des références aux manuscrits et matériaux dans archives. c.r.: *University of Toronto Quarterly* 50/4 Summer 1981 206-8 (J.T. Stevenson), *Cahiers du Cap-Rouge* 812 1980 75-7 (Jean-Paul Tremblay), *Dialogue* 20/3 1981 600-2 (Louise Marcil-Lacoste), *Livres et Auteurs Québécois* 1980 295-6, *Prospectives* 17/3 OC1981 159-60 (J.-P. Tremblay), *Recherches Sociographiques* 22/2 MA-AU1981 287-8 (Nadia Fahmy-Eid), *Revue d'- Histoire de l'Amerique Française* 35/2 SE1981 278-81 (Louise Marcil-Lacoste).

221 Yvan Lamonde, "Philosophies et philosophes européens au Québec (XVIIe-XXe siècle)." *La Communication*, Tome I. Actes du XVe Congrès de l'Association des Sociétés de Philosophie de Langue Française. Montréal: Editions Montmorency, 1971.

222 Yvan Lamonde, "Pour une tradition critique." *Critère* no. 10 JA1974 147-50.

223 Albert-Marie Landry, "Louis-Marie Régis, o.p. Quelques dates et faits marquants de sa vie." *La scolastique. En hommage à Louis-Marie Régis*. Ed. par Ernest Joos. Montréal: Bellarmin 1980. 201-6. Bibliographie 204-6. Régis, professeur de la philosophie à l'Université de Montréal, est un personnage influentiel chez les philosophes catholiques de l'Etats-Unis.

224 Albert-Marie Landry, "La pensée philosophique médiévale. Contribution canadienne (1960-1973)." *Philosophiques* 1 OC1974 111-39. Renseégne ouvrages publiés en Canada par non- canadiens aussi bien que publications par canadiens.

225 Paul-Emile Langevin, "Hommage à Emmanuel Trepanier," par P.-E. Langevin & Michel Ponton. *Laval Théologique et Philosophique* 39/1 FE1983 3-6.

226 Jean Langlois, "Une lecture de la philosophie québécoise." *Critère* no. 6-7 SE1972 373-88.

227 Jean Langlois, "Le mouvement automatiste et la philosophie contemporaine au Québec." *Science et Esprit* 25/2 1973 225-53.

228 Jean Langlois, "La philosophie au Canada français." *Sciences Ecclésiastiques* 10/1 JA1958 95-105.

229 Jean Langlois, "Le rôle de la philosophie dans la culture canadienne." *Dialogue* 1/2 1962 117-28.

230 Antoinette La Salle-Leduc, "La Société d'Etude et des Conférences." *Revue Dominicaine* 42/1 1936 46-8.

231   François Latraverse, "Les études wittgensteiniennes au Canada; état de la recherche." *Philosophiques* 12/1 Printemps 1985 197-209. Recensement selon les catégories: articles; articles partiellement consacrés à Wittgenstein; monographies, ouvrages collectifs; monographies partiellement consacrées...; mémoires et thèses; conférences et communications; recherches; enseignements.

232   André Lavalée, *La querelle universitaire 1876-1891, Québec contre Montréal.* Préf. de Philippe Sylvain, Montréal: Les Presses de l'Université de Montréal, 1974. 288p. La lutte pour une université indépendante à Montréal fut un developpement important dans l'histoire de la culture du Québec.

233   Marc Lebel, "L'enseignement de la philosophie." *Aspects de l'enseignement au Petit Seminaire de Québec* (1765- 1945). Québec: Société Historique de Québec, 1968. (Société Historique de Québec, no. 20) 11-77.

234   Marc Lebel, *L'enseignement de la philosophie au Petit Seminaire de Québec 1765-1880.* Thèse de maîtrise (Histoire). Université Laval, 1964. xiv, 125p.

235   Marc Lebel, "L'époque de Jérôme Demers 1800-1850." *Aspects de l'enseignement au Petit Seminaire de Québec 1765-1845.* Québec: La Société Historique de Québec, 1968. 31-60.

236   M. Lebel & W. Lamb, *Thèses des gradués canadiens dans les humanités et les sciences sociales: 1921-1940.* Ottawa: Imprimerie de le Roi, 1951. Section philosophique p.157- 78.

237   Lucien Lelièvre, *L'enseignement du thomisme dans les collèges classiques.* Montréal: Fides, 1965. (Philosophie et problèmes contemporaines). 241p. Bibliographie p.235-7. Discussion normative de l'enseignement de la philosophie au Québec. Thèse du doctorat, Institut Catholique de Paris, 1962.

238   Lucien Lelièvre, "L'enseignement de la philosophie thomiste dans les collèges secondaires du Canada- Français." *Revue des Sciences Philosophiques et Théologiques* 48/3 JL1963 480f.

239   Lucien Lelièvre, "L'enseignement du thomisme dans les collèges classiques." *Collège et Famille* 23/1 1966 23-33.

240   Edmour Lemay, "La philosophie à l'Université de Montréal." *Culture* 3/3 SE1942 381-3.

241   Hugolin Lemay, *Bibliographie franciscaine. Inventaire des revues, livres, brochures et autres écrits publiés par les Franciscains du Canada de*

1890 à 1915. par R.P. Hugolin. Québec: Imprimerie Franciscaine Missionaire, 1916. 143p. *Supplément jusqu'à l'année 1931.* Québec: Imprimerie Franciscaine Missionaire, 1932. 214p.

242 Hugolin Lemay, *Bio-bibliographie du R.P. Ephrem Longpré, o.f.m.* Par R.P. Hugolin. Québec: Imprimerie Franciscaine Missionaire, 1931. 40p. Bibliographie p.17- 40. Les écrits de Longpré jusqu'à 1930 avec listes des "Travaux...en cours d'impression" et travaux "en préparation," avec citations des commentaires sur Longpré, description du contenu des écrits de Longpré et remarques sur leur reception.

243 Hugolin Lemay, "Etude bibliographique et historique sur la *Morale pratique* du jansenisme du P. Louis Hennepin, recollet." *Mémoires de la Société Royale du Canada* 1937 sect. 1 127-49. Hennepin fut missionaire en Nouvelle France, explorateur de la cascade de Niagara.

244 Victor Levin, "History of the department of philosophy, McGill University, 1940-1970." by Victor Levin and Laura Zagolin. *Matériaux pour l'histoire des institutions de philosophie au Québec.* Québec: Presses de l'Université Laval, 1976. (Cahiers de l'Institut Supérieur des Sciences Humaines, No. 4 T.1.) 287-369.

245 "A list of publications by John Watson." *Douglas Library Notes* 16/4 Summer 1968 8-14. List arranged chronologically. Accompanies "A sketch of Professor Watson." p.4-7.

246 Douglas Grant Lochhead, *Bibliographie des bibliographies canadiennes/ Bibliography of Canadian bibliographies.* 2 ed. Index by Peter Greig. Toronto: University of Toronto Press, 1972. xiv, 312p. With author and subject indexes.

247 Rupert Clendon Lodge, "Comments II." *Philosophy in Canada, a symposium.* By John A. Irving, *et al.* Toronto: University of Toronto Press, 1952. 44-8.

248 Rupert Clendon Lodge, "Philosophy as taught in the University of Manitoba." *Culture* 2/4 DC1941 430-4.

249 John Daniel Logan, *Aesthetic criticism in Canada; its aims, methods and status*, by Novicius Aloysius (pseud.), Toronto: McClelland, 1917. 29p. Logan was trained in philosophy and literary criticism. He later moved to Vermilion, South Dakota where he became professor of English literature, and then returned to Toronto where he worked in advertising.

250 Anselme Longpré, *Ephrem Longpré 1890-1965.* Québec: Bibliothèque Nationale de Québec, 1974. 121p. Bibliographie par Edouard Parent, 105-21.

251   André Loranger, *Proposition plans-cadres: rapport final du projet pédagogique*, par André Loranger & Pierre Girouard. Tracy: Département de philosophie, Cégep Sorel-Tracy, 1983. 61f. fac sim Rel. a spirale. Sur l'enseignement de la philosophie au niveau collégial.

252   A.R.M. Lower, "The social sciences in Canada." *Culture* 3 1942 433-40.

253   Edmund J. McCorkell, *Henry Carr - revolutionary*. Toronto: Griffin House, 1969. 165p. Carr was a philosophy professor at St Michael's College in Toronto and a noteworthy administrator. He was largely responsible for the organisation of the Pontifical Institute of Mediaeval Studies and for the invitation of Etienne Gilson to Toronto.

254   John McCumber, "Hegel: life, letters and system." *Queen's Quarterly* 93/3 Aut1986 637-44. A review of an edition and translation of Hegel's letters with comments on Canadian Hegel scholarship and its milieu, p.642f.

255   Michael McDonald, "Philosophy in Canada." *Dialogue* 25/1 Spring 1986 3-4. Introduction, by the anglophone editor, to the 25th anniversary issue of *Dialogue*.

256   J.M. MacEachran, "John Watson (1847-1939)." *Some great men of Queen's*. Ed. by Robert Charles Wallace. Toronto: Ryerson, 1941. 22-50. Brief bibliography p.50. Watson was the great and prolific philosophy professor at Queen's during the later 19th and early 20th Centuries. An idealist in the tradition of Caird, he had greater international academic influence than any of his English- Canadian colleagues.

257 Margaret McGrath, *Etienne Gilson, a bibliography/Etienne Gilson, une bibliographie*. Toronto: Pontifical Institute of Mediaeval Studies, 1982. xxviii, 124p. An extensive bibliography of both primary and secondary sources in bilingual format. Compressed presentation with some analysis and annotation. c.r.: *Papers of the Bibliographical Society of Canada* 21 1982 95-6 (Carl Spadoni); *Review of Metaphysics* 38/1 1984 132-3 (Jude Dougherty).

258   A. Brian McKillop, *A critical spirit, the thought of William Dawson LeSueur*. Ed. A. Brian McKillop. Toronto: McClelland and Stewart, 1977. 317p. A collection of writings with an introductory essay p.xii-xxiii, and section introductions by McKillop. Contains an extensive bibliography of LeSueur p.314-17. Bibliographical notes. c.r.: *Dialogue* 18/4 DC1979 616-9 (Anthony Rasporich)..

259 A. Brian McKillop, *A disciplined intelligence. Critical inquiry and Canadian thought in the Victorian era.* Montreal: McGill-Queen's University Press, 1979. xii, 287p. Bibliographic notes p. 235-278. A thorough survey of nineteenth-century Canadian views on philosophic and related topics. It argues that many figures of the period believed that critical pursuits ought to be subservient to certain moral values.

260 A. Brian McKillop, "John Watson and the idealist legacy." *Canadian Literature* 83 Winter 1979 72-88.

261 A. Brian McKillop, *Speculative idealism and the social gospel in Canada.* Unpublished talk delivered at Queen's University. 29p. Bibliographical footnotes. Copy available in the office of Bibliography of Philosophy in Canada. Covers much of the same ground as no. 221 and the final chapter of no. 220.

262 Alastair Mackinnon, "Les études Kierkegaardiennes au Canada." *Philosophiques* 9/1 AL1982 147-61.

263 T.P. McLaughlin, "General index of *Mediaeval Studies*, vol. 1-25 (1939-1963)." *Mediaeval Studies* 26 1964. *Mediaeval Studies* is an annual publication of international importance, published by the Pontifical Institute of Mediaeval Studies, Toronto.

264 George F. McLean, *Philosophy in the twentieth century: Catholic and Christian.* Ed. George F. McLean. New York: Ungar, 1976. 2 vols. 683p. with an annotated bibliography of religious philosophy, an appendix listing doctoral dissertations in philosophy presented in Catholic universities in the U.S. and Canada, and extensive indexes.

265 R.D. MacLennan, "Philosophy and liberal education." *Culture* 2/4 1941 422-4. Includes comments on philosophy at McGill.

266 Cyrus MacMillan, *McGill and its story, 1821-1921.* London: John Lane & Toronto: Oxford University Press, Canadian Branch, 1921. xiv, 304p. Mainly an institutional history. Contains a chapter on Sir William Dawson.

267 Don MacNiven, "A code of ethics for Canadian philosophers: a working paper," by Don MacNiven, Philip MacEwan & Cidalia Paiva. *Dialogue* 25/1 Spring 1986 179-89. Reports on and discusses the results of a questionnaire on professional ethics for philosophers circulated by the Occupational Ethics Group (Toronto) to Canadian philosophers.

268 Crawford Brough Macpherson, "The position of political science." *Culture* 3 1942 452-9.

269   A. Maheu, "Pierre Stanislas Bédard, 1763-1829: philosophe et savant." *Mémoires de la Société Royale du Canada* 50/sect. 2 1956 85-93. Sur l'éditeur du *Le Canadien.* cf. la biographie par N.-E. Dionne, "Pierre Bédard et son temps." *Mémoires de la Société Royale du Canada*, série 2 4/sect. 1 1898 73-117.

270   Louis Maheu, "Nationalismes et nationalisation du champ scientifique québécoise." *Sociologie et Sociétés* 7/2 1975 89-114.

271   Arthur Maheux, "The origins of Laval University." *Canadian Historical Association, Annual Report* 1952 22-7.

272   Louise Marcil-Lacoste, "Essai en philosophie: problematique pour l'établissement d'un corpus." *Philosophiques* 13/1 Printemps 1986 65-111. Bibliographie 93-111.   Repr *L'Essai et la prose d'idées au Québec.* Montréal: Fides, 1985. 211-42 ("Archives des lettres canadiennes," t.6). Sur l'essai philosophique en lettres canadiennes-française; analyse des prétextes pour l'exclusion des matériaux de la catégorie "philosophie."

273   Louise Marcil-Lacoste, *La logique judiciare de Maximilien Bibaud* Ms 10p. Exemplaire dans le bureau de la Bibliographie de la Philosophie au Canada.

274   Louise Marcil-Lacoste, "La situation institutionelle de la philosophie au Québec." *Bulletin de la Société de la Philosophie au Québec* 2 1976 29-38.

275   Louise Marcil-Lacoste, "Le régard de l'autre: la philosophie et l'émergence des sciences sociales." *Continuité et rupture--les sciences sociales au Québec.* Montréal: Presses de l'Université de Montréal, 1984. 435-54.

276   Jacques Marcoux, "Le Collège Dominicain d'Ottawa." *Communauté Chrétienne* 12/70 1973 314-20.

277   Soeur Marie-de-St. Didier (Sr. du Bon Pasteur), *Bibliographie de Mgr. Henri Grenier.* Québec: U. Laval, thèse de bibliothéconomie, 1948.

278   (Soeur) Marie-Germaine, *Psychologie rationelle au Canada français, bibliographie* (1945-1963). Québec: Université Laval, Ecole de Bibliothéconomie, 1964. 60p.

279   Soeur Marie-Raymond, *Bio-bibliographie du R.P. Georges Simard.* Par une religieuse des Saints Noms de Jesus et de Marie. Montréal: Beauchemin, 1939. 68p.

280   Jacques Maritain, *Etienne Gilson, philosophe de la chrétienté.* Par Jacques Maritain *et al.* Paris: Editions du Cerf, 1949. (Rencontres No. 30) 295p. "Vie et oeuvres" p.13-21.

281 Jacques Martineau, "L'enseignement de la philosophie et le livre blanc sur les collèges du Québec." *Prospectives* 16/4 DC1980 168-72.

282 D.C. Masters, "The ideological background." *Protestant church colleges in Canada: a history.* Toronto: University of Toronto Press, 1966. p.3-16.

283 Thomas Mathien, "The natural history of philosophy in Canada." *Dialogue* 25/1 Spring 1986 53-65. A sceptical examination of several ways of characterizing philosophy in Canada. Based on a presentation at the C.P.A. meetings, Montreal, 1985. cf. no. 5.

284 *Mélanges à la mémoire de Charles de Koninck.* Québec: Presses de l'Université Laval, 1968. Bibliographie de Charles de Koninck par A. Gagné, p.7-22. Avec références bibliographiques.

285 Jean-Guy Meunier, "Le livre blanc de 'La politique québécoise de développement culturel.' Esquisse critique d'une philosophie de la culture." *Philosophiques* 6/2 OC1979 347-60.

286 Hugo Meynell, "Aspects of the philosophy of Kai Nielsen." *Dialogue* 25/1 Spring 1986 83-92. On the work of a prolific Canadian writer on ethics, political philosophy and philosophy of religion.

287 A.M. Mignault, *La résistance aux lois injustes et la doctrine catholique.* Montréal: L'Action Française, 1921. Avec, en appendice, listes des livres, brochures,...publiés par les Pères Dominicains de la province du Canada.

288 Judy Mills, *University of Toronto doctoral theses, (1897- 1967).* by Judy Mills and Irene Dombra. Toronto: University of Toronto Press, 1968. Section on dissertations in philosophy, p.98-108. A noteworthy list of dissertations in philosophy. In the period covered, the majority were prepared for professors associated with the Pontifical Institute of Mediaeval Studies.

289 Denis Monière, *Le développement des idéologies au Québec: des origines à nos jours.* Ottawa: Editions Québec/Amérique, 1977. 381p. Bibliographie, p.379-81.

290 Denis Monière, *Les idéologies au Québec: bibliographie.* Par Denis Monière & André Vachet. Montréal: Bibliothèque Nationale du Québec, 1976. 2 ed. rev. & aug., 1977. 3 ed. rev. & aug., 1980. 173p. Disponible chez la Bibliothèque Nationale du Québec. Contient inventaire des sources bibliographiques, liste alphabetisée par nom d'auteur & index analytique.

291 Denis Monière, *Ideologies in Quebec: the historical development.* Tr. by Richard Howard. Toronto: University of Toronto Press, 1981. 328p.

Includes bibliographical references. Tr. of *Le développement...* c.r.: *Dialogue* 22/1 MR1983 163-6 (J.T. Stevenson).

292   Luis Morfin, "Du dépassement comme devoir quotidien." *Relations* 40/456 FE1980. Du Bernard Lonergan à l'occasion de son 75e anniversaire. Fait référence à son interêt actuel dans le domaine de l'économie politique.

293   Jacques Morissette, "Descartes et la destin de la philosophie au Québec." *Discours de la méthode et autres textes.* par René Descartes, Ed. Jacques Morissette. Présentation, chronologie et notes par Jacques Morissette. Montréal: Hexagone-Minerve, 1981. (Collection: Balises 1) 161-7.

294   Christopher W. Morris, "Marxism in Quebec: demise or rebirth." *Dialogue* 23/3 SE1984 475-80. On Maurice Lagueux, *Le marxisme des années soixante* (no. 210).

295   V.V. Mshvenieradze, "Early Canadian philosophers: a Soviet view." *The Marxist Quarterly* no. 1 Spring 1962 65- 75. Trans. & reprint of part of a chapter of *Istoria Filosofi* vol. 5. Moscow: Institute of Philosophy, U.S.S.R. Academy of Sciences, 1961.

296   C.R. Myers, "Notes on the history of psychology in Canada." *The Canadian Psychologist* 6a/1 JA1965 4-19. In the 19th and early 20th centuries, psychology was often taught in close conjunction with philosophy. The author provides interesting information on that connection.

297   Marcel Nadeau, "'La philosophie au Québec'--Echos de la vingt-cinquième rencontre du CGM." *Bulletin du Cercle Gabriel Marcel* 1/3 JN1979 20-1.

298   Robert Nadeau, "Hommage à Hugues Leblanc, philosophe, logicien." *Philosophiques* 13/1 Printemps 1986 131-45. "Hugues Leblanc: bibliographie (1949-85)" 138-45. Sur un logicien aux E.-U., né et formé au Québec.

299   Hilda Neatby, *Queen's University,* 2 vols.: vol. 1 *1841- 1917, To strive to seek, to find and not to yield* by Hilda Neatby. vol. 2 *1917-1961. To serve and yet be free* by Frederick Gibson. Kingston & Montreal: McGill-Queen's University Press, 1978-1983. Vol. 1 contains discussion of Murray, Watson and their role at Queen's, and deals with the controversy which dogged Professor James George. Vol. 2 has brief comments on George Humphrey and Gregory Vlastos. Both volumes contain bibliographies.

300   Robin Neill, *A new theory of value: the Canadian economics of H.A. Innis.* Toronto: University of Toronto Press, 1972. 159p. Includes a revised version of Jane Ward's bibliography of Innis (No. 398), p. 27-45.

301 David Fate Norton, *The Scottish enlightenment exported: John Clark Murray (1836-1917)*. Communication presented at Learned Societies meetings, Fredericton, N.B., 1977. Murray was professor of philosophy at McGill, an idealist, and a commentator on social as well as purely philosophical issues.

302 *Notices en langue française du Canadian catalog of Books, 1921-1949* vol. 12. Index par H.B. Boivin, Québec: Bibliothèque Nationale du Québec, 1975. 263p. & index. L'index inclu, *inter alia*, une liste des publications par Damien Jasmin.

303 J. Reginald O'Donnell, "Anton Charles Pegis--on the occasion of his retirement." *Essays in honour of Anton Charles Pegis*. Ed. J.R. O'Donnell, Toronto: Pontifical Institute of Mediaeval Studies, 1974. p. 7-16. With extensive but not exhaustive bibliography of Pegis. Until his death in 1978, Pegis was associated with the Pontifical Institute and worked on Thomistic philosophical anthropology and on theories of intentionality.

304 J. Reginald O'Donnell, "Joseph Thomas Muckle 1887-1967." *Mediaeval Studies* 29 1967 v-viii. Bibliography p. vi-vii. Muckle was a mediaevalist writing on topics of philosophic interest.

305 Joan O'Donovan, *George Grant and the twilight of justice*. Toronto: University of Toronto Press, 1984. ix, 196p. Bibliography: Published writings of Grant, 181-5; Selected writings on Grant, 185. An account, by a theologian, of George Grant's intellectual development and current concerns in social theory.

306 Rejean Olivier, *Vie de l'abbé Frédéric-Alexandre, notre polygraphe québécois*. Joliette: Edition privée, 1977. 110p.

307 Joseph Owens, *The philosophical tradition of St. Michael's College*. Toronto: University of St. Michael's College Archives, 1979. 40p. Bibliographical footnotes. Includes a discussion of subjects taught and textbooks employed, and illustrations of text-book title pages.

308 *The Oxford companion to canadian literature*. Ed. W. Toye. Toronto: Oxford University Press, 1983. Contains a discussion of "Philosophy in Canada" by Leslie Armour and Elizabeth Trott, p.642-7, as well as entries by Armour, Trott and others on Jacques Brault, Charles De Koninck, Jérôme Demers, Rodolphe Dubé, Northrop Frye, Fernand Dumont, Louis Lachance, Rupert C. Lodge, William Lyall, John Clark Murray, W.D. Lightall, L.-A. Pâquet and Francis Sparshott. Passing references are made elsewhere to a number of other Canadian philosophers.

309 Willard Gurndon Oxtoby, "Bibliography of Wilfred Cantwell- Smith." *Religious diversity; essays of W.C. Smith.* Ed. Willard Gurndon Oxtoby. New York: Harper & Row, 1976. 185-94. W.C. Smith is a theologian interested in philosophic and comparative issues.

310 F. Hilton Page, *The origins and development of psychology at Dalhousie University.* Unpublished paper by F. Hilton Page and James Clark. 1981 (?) 16p. Copy in office of the Bibliography of Philosophy in Canada.

311 F. Hilton Page, *Recollections of G.S. Brett: continuity in Canadian philosophy.* A paper read at the Conference on Philosophy in Canada at the University of Ottawa, March 9, 1979. 18p. Copy in office of the Bibliography of Philosophy in Canada.

312 F. Hilton Page, *William Lyall and the abyss of nihilism.* A paper read at the 25th annual congress of the Canadian Philosophical Association at Dalhousie University, May 29, 1981. 19p. Accompanied by a 1p. "Summary of Lyall's philosophy." Lyall was Professor of Logic and Philosophy at Dalhousie University 1863-1890. Available, office of the Bibliography of Philosophy in Canada, Department of Philosophy University of Toronto.

313 F. Hilton Page, "William Lyall in his setting." *Dalhousie Review* 60 1980 49-66.

314 Leslie Pal, "Scholarship and the later Innis." *Journal of Canadian Studies* 12/5 Winter 1977.

315 Claude Panaccio, "Marxisme et rationalité scientifique." *Dialogue* 23/3 SE1984 481-91. Sur *Le marxisme des années soixante* par Maurice Lagueux (no. 210).

316 Claude Panaccio, *Philosophie au Québec.* Ed. par Claude Panaccio & P.-A. Quintin. Montréal: Bellarmin, & Paris: Desclée de Brouwer, 1976. 263p. (Collection, "L'Univers de la Philosophie," 5). c.r.: L'*Information Médicale et Paramédicale* 29/18 2AU1977 21 (Jean-Pierre Légaré).

317 Claude Panaccio, "Table Ronde sur le positivisme: introduction anecdotique." *Bulletin de la Société de Philosophie du Québec* 6/1 1980 74-81. Sur le développement de l'interêt dans la philosophie "positiviste" au Québec. cfr. no. 157.

318 Antonin Papillon, "Pour l'histoire du thomisme au Canada." *Revue Dominicaine* 33 OC1927 538-46.

319 Louis-Adolphe Pâquet, "Coup d'oeil sur l'histoire de l'enseignement de la philosophie traditionelle au Canada." *Mémoires de la Société Royale* *du Canada* 3e série 11 1917 37-60. Repr. en version augmentée *Mélanges canadiens*. Par L.-A. Pâquet. Québec: 1918. 141-207.

320 André Paradis, *Bibliographie sur la préhistoire de la psychiatrie canadienne au 19e. siècle*. Comp. par André Paradis, Viateur Dubé, Alain Fugére & Jean Lafrance. Trois-Rivières: Université du Québec à Trois-Rivières, Département de Philosophie, 1976. xii, 118p. (Collection: Recherches et Théories).

321 André Paradis, *Essais pour une préhistoire de la psychiatrie au Canada (1800-1885)*. Par André Paradis, Viateur Dubé, Alain Fugére & Jean Lafrance. Suivi d'une anthologie de textes. Trois-Rivières: Université du Québec à Trois-Rivières, 1977. vii, 346p. (Collection: Recherches et Théories).

322 Gilles Paradis, "La documentation en philosophie: bibliographies courantes." *Philosophiques* 6/1 AL1979 177- 99.

323 Edouard Parent, "Bibliographie du P(ère) Ephrem Longpré, o.f.m." *Culture* 27 SE1966 276-89.

324 Edouard Parent, *Ephrem Longpré, un mystique franciscain de notre temps: Journal spirituel et lettres*. Paris: Beauchesne, 1969. 323p. (Bibliothèque de spiritualité, 7). c.r.: *Dialogue* 8/3 DC1969 531-2 (Yvan Lamonde).

325 Edouard Parent, "Un médiéviste canadien-français." *Dialogue* 6/4 1968 486-96. Avec bibliographie de Longpré, p.490-6.

326 Desirée Park, "Bibliography of Raymond Klibansky." By Desirée Park & Michael J. Whalley. *Revue Internationale de Philosophie* 29 1975 167-74. The work of Park and Whalley on Klibansky, noted McGill professor, should be used carefully. It contains a number of misleading references.

327 Desirée Park, "Bibliography of Raymond Klibansky's writings." By Desirée Park, Michael J. Whalley & H. Kohlenberger. *Reason, action and experience. Essays in honour of Raymond Klibansky*. Ed. Helmut Kohlenberger. Hamburg: Meiner, 1979. 243-50.

328 Morton Paterson, *The letters and papers of G.J. Blewett*. Presented at the Conference on Philosophy in Canada, 9MR1979. 43p. A bio-bibliographic discussion of a promising thinker whose life was cut short by accidental death (1912). Available, office of the Bibliography of Philosophy in Canada, Department of Philosophy, University of Toronto.

329   Graeme Patterson, "Harold Innis and the writing of history." *Canadian Literature* no. 83 Winter 1979 118-30.

330   Gerald B. Phelan, "The teaching of philosophy in non- Catholic universities in Canada." *L'Academie Canadienne St.-Thomas d'Aquin.* 3e session (12 & 13 octobre 1932). Québec: Typ. L'Action Catholique, 1934. 85-115.

331   Stanley Pinteric, *A bibliography of the works of Francis Edward Sparshott.* Toronto: submitted 10AL1979. A typescript prepared by a student in the Faculty of Library Science, University of Toronto. Unpaginated copy in the office of the Bibliography of Philosophy in Canada, Department of Philosophy, University of Toronto.

332 Jacques Plamondon, *The current state of philosophy in Quebec.* Paper read at the Edmonton meetings of the Western Canadian Philosophical Association, OC1973. 8p. A rather simplified treatment of philosophy in Quebec. Available, office of the Bibliography of Philosophy in Canada, Department of Philosophy, University of Toronto.

333 J. Antonin Plourde, *Dominicains au Canada. Livre des documents I. La foundation canadienne à Saint-Hyacinthe (1830-1886).* Montréal: Editions du Lévrier, 1973. 539p. Saint-Hyacinthe fut le centre de la naissance du Thomisme au Québec.

334   Marthe Plourde, *Bio-bibliographie de M. l'abbé L.-E. Otis.* Québec: Université Laval, thèse de bibliothéconomie, 1964. 35p.

335   Simonne Plourde, "Présence de la pensée de Gabriel Marcel au Canada (1940-1978)." *Philosophiques* 6/1 AL1979 147-73. Discussion de la contribution canadienne à l'étude de la pensée de Marcel. Inclu abstraits des articles scolaires et thèses sur Marcel et une liste de thèses canadiennes sur sa philosophie.

336 Michael Pomedli, "The concept of 'soul' in the Jesuit Relations: were there any philosophers among the North American Indians?" *Laval Théologique et Philosophique* 41/1 FE1985 57-64. Résumé en français, 57. A discussion of Jesuit attributions of doctrines of "soul" to native North American informants; raises important questions about indigenous N. American ideology and about the nature of philosophy.

337   Gonzalve Poulin, "L'enseignement des sciences sociales dans les universités canadiennes." *Culture* 2 1941 338-49. L'auteur compare l'institutionnalisation des sciences sociales au Québec et au Canada anglais.

338   Honorius Provost, *Historique de la Faculté des Arts de l'Université Laval, 1852-1952.* Québec: L'Enseignement Secondaire au Canada, 1952. vi, 203p. Avec une liste alphabetique des professeurs dans la Faculté des Arts de 1852 à 1952. La Faculté des Arts de Laval établit les examens en philosophie pour le baccalaureat dans les collèges classiques au Québec.

339   Honorius Provost, *Le Seminaire de Québec. Documents et biographies.* Québec: Presses Universitaires Laval, 1964. xviii, 542p.

340   John Douglas Rabb, "Canadian idealism, philosophical federalism, and world peace." *Dialogue* 25/1 Spring 1986 93-103. Claims that a number of Canadian thinkers have, as a result of a typically Canadian view of reason as a means of reconciling differences, developed social theories which recommend world federalism.

341   John Douglas Rabb, "The fusion philosophy of Crawford-Frost." *Idealistic Studies* 16/1 Spring 1986 77-92. On an obscure but interesting Canadian thinker of late 19th and early 20th centuries.

342   John Douglas Rabb, *Religion and reason: a symposium.* Ed. with an introduction by J. Douglas Rabb. Winnipeg: Frye Publishing Co., 1983. xvii, 116p. "Memorial volume...dedicated to the memory of William Sparkes Morris, priest and scholar." Symposium held 3-17MR1982 at Lakehead University, Thunder Bay, Ont. Includes bibliographical references. Contains an essay by Rabb entitled "Reason and revelation revisited: a Canadian perspective." p.2-19. c.r.: *Dialogue* 25/1 Spring 1986 195-8 (Elmer John Thiessen).

343   Mark Rabnett, *A bibliography of Emil L. Fackenheim.* Toronto: 1979. Typescript prepared by a student in the Faculty of Library Science, University of Toronto. It includes secondary as well as primary material, and abstracts of Fackenheim's books. Available, office of the Bibliography of Philosophy in Canada, Department of Philosophy, University of Toronto.

344   Jean Racette, "Faire évoluer notre enseignement de la philosophie." *Collège et Famille* FE1963 1-15.

345   Jean Racette, "La philosophie au Canada français." *Dialogue* 3/3 DC1964 288-98.

346   Jean Racette, "La philosophie dans les collèges autrefois dits classiques." *Relations* no. 314 1967 66-9.

347   Jean Racette, *Thomisme ou pluralisme, réflexions sur l'enseignement de la philosophie.* Préf. de Jean LaCroix. Montréal: Bellarmin, & Paris: Desclée de Brouwer, 1967. (Essais pour notre temps, section de philosophie, 8) Avec notes bibliographiques.

348   Louis-Marie Régis, "La philosophie au Canada français." *Communauté Chrétienne* 12/70 JL-AU1973 261-70.

349 *Register of post-graduate dissertations in progress in history and related subjects/Répertoire des thèses en cours portant sur des sujets d'histoire et autres sujets connexes.* Comp. Public Archives of Canada. Pub. Canadian Historical Association/Société Historique du Canada. Issued annually since 1966. Includes useful sections on historiography, intellectual history, history of science and technology.

350 Arthur Robert, *Catalogues pour bibliothèques de classe. Philosophie.* Montréal: 1915. Signalise des ouvrages consultés par professeurs de la philosophie dans le temps de l'auteur.

351 Lucie Robert, *Discours critique et discours historique dans le Manuel d'histoire de la littérature canadienne de langue française de Mgr. Camille Roy.* Thèse publiée par l'Institut Québécois de Recherche sur la Culture, 1982.

352   Patrice Robert, "Les franciscaines canadiens et les études médiévales." *Chronique Franciscaine du Canada* 2 MA1941 59-100.

353   Wayne Roberts, "Goldwin's myth." (on Goldwin Smith) *Canadian Literature* no. 83 Winter 1979 50-71. Includes extensive bibliography. Probes the received view of Smith as "Victorian liberal."

354 Gilbert de Beauregard Robinson, *The mathematics department in the University of Toronto 1827-1978.* Toronto: University of Toronto Press, 1979. Includes discussion of Paxton Young's mathematics papers and of a number of mathematics professors who had some influence on Toronto philosophers.

355 Peter Noble Ross, *The origins and development of the Ph.D. degree at the University of Toronto, 1871-1932.* Toronto: 1972. xii, 381 l. Bibliography, leaves 356-8. Unpublished thesis, University of Toronto.

356 César Rouben, "Propagande antiphilosophique dans les gazettes de Montréal et de Québec après la fin du régime français." *Revue de l'Université d'Ottawa* 54/3 JL-SE1984 79-98. Avec annexes bibliographiques p. 91-8.

357 Gérard Roulet, "Un bilan du marxisme." *Philosophiques* 13/1 Printemps 1986 147-52. Etude critique du *Le marxisme des années 60*, par Maurice Lagueux (no. 210). Avec réponse par Lagueux, "Un "bilan" vite parcouru," 153-5.

358 Louis Rousseau, *La théologie québécoise contemporaine (1940-1973): genèse de ses productions et transformations de son discours.* Québec:

Université Laval, Institut Superieur des Sciences Humaines 1977. (Etudes sur Québec, no. 8) 162p.

359 Maurice Roy, "Pour l'histoire du thomisme au Canada." *Journées thomistes vol. I: Essais et bilans.* Ottawa: Collège Dominicain 1935, 17-28.

360 Maurice Roy, "Pour l'histoire du thomisme au Canada." *Canada-Français* 23 1935 161-71.

361 Jacques Ruelland, "Philosophie et ordinateur." *Critère* 41 Printemps 1986 135-43. Sur l'enseignement de la philosophie par ordinateur à Cégep.

362 Dagobert D. Runes, *Who's who in philosophy.* Ed. Dagobert Runes, Lester E. Dennon & Ralph B. Winn. New York: Philosophical Library, 1942.

363 Jean-Claude St.-Amant, "La propaganda de l'Ecole Sociale Populaire en faveur du syndicalisme catholique 1911-1949." *Revue de l'Histoire de l'Amérique Française* 32/2 SE1978 203-28. Considère un aspect de la pensée sociale catholique et un mouvement important au Québec.

364 Robert J. L. Scollard, *Basilian fathers: short account of the history, life and works of the Congregation of St. Basil.* Toronto: Basilian Press, 1940. 32p.

365 Wilfred Senécal, "L'enseignement de la philosophie dans nos collèges classiques." *Journées thomistes, vol. I. Essais et bilans.* Ottawa: Collège Dominicain, 1935. 95- 103.

366 Laurence K. Shook, *Catholic post-secondary education in English-speaking Canada.* Toronto: University of Toronto Press, 1971. x, 457p. Includes articles on St. Michael's College, the Pontifical Institute of Mediaeval Studies, St. Augustine's Seminary, Assumption College in Windsor, etc.

367 Laurence K. Shook, *Etienne Gilson.* Toronto: Pontifical Institute of Mediaeval Studies, 1984. x, 412p. Bibliographical notes and index. (Etienne Gilson Series, no. 6) Biography of Gilson with extensive discussion of his role in Canada.

368 S.E.D. Shortt, *The search for an ideal. Six Canadian intellectuals and their convictions in an age of transition.* Toronto: University of Toronto Press, 1976. viii, 216p. Contains an extensive bibliography of writings, many of which have at least peripheral philosophic relevance, p. 183-212.

369 Georges Simard, "Pénétration effective de la philosophie dans les esprits et dans la société." *Culture* 2/4 DC1941 426-30. Sur l'enseignement de la philosophie à l'Université d'Ottawa.

370   Société des Ecrivains Canadiens, *Répertoire bio- bibliographique de la Société des Ecrivains Canadiens.* Montréal: Editions de la Société, 1954.

371   Francis Edward Sparshott, "National philosophy." *Dialogue* 16/1 MR1977 3-21. Presidential address to the Canadian Philosophical Association, 1976. A critical discussion of a nationalist approach to philosophy in Canada and especially of the treatment in T.H.B. Symons' report on Canadian Studies, no. 381.

372   John Torrance Stevenson, "Canadian philosophy from a cosmopolitan point of view." *Dialogue* 25/1 Spring 1986 17-30. Answers a series of objections to the study of the history of philosophy in Canada, and presents a case for its value. Development of 373.

373   John Torrance Stevenson, *On the philosophy of the history of national philosophy.* Unpublished paper delivered to the Conference on Canadian Philosophy, Ottawa, 9MR1979. 19p. Bibliographical notes. Available, office of the Bibliography of Philosophy in Canada, Department of Philosophy, University of Toronto.

374   John Torrance Stevenson, *Some reflections on "National philosophy".* Typescript 28p. A response to Sparshott (no. 371). Available, office of the Bibliography of Philosophy in Canada, Department of Philosophy, University of Toronto. This paper was delivered, Canadian Philosophical Association meetings. Fredericton, 1977.

375   John Torrance Stevenson, *Bibliography of Rupert Clendon Lodge.* Available, office of the Bibliography of Philosophy in Canada, Department of Philosophy, University of Toronto. Lodge was the major philosopher at the University of Manitoba for many years, and a Plato scholar.

376   L. Wayne Sumner, *Pragmatism and purpose: essays presented to Thomas A. Goudge.* Ed. L. Wayne Sumner, John G. Slater and Fred Wilson. Toronto: University of Toronto Press, 1981. Bibliography: "The published works of Thomas A. Goudge," p.329-36.

377   Victor Svacek, "Crawford Brough Macpherson: a bibliography." *Powers, possessions and freedoms. Essays in honour of C.B. Macpherson.* Ed. Alkis Kontos. Toronto: University of Toronto Press, 1979. p.167-78. A bibliography to Sept. 1979 of the works of the famous Canadian political thinker. Includes some annotations and some references to secondary material.

378   Philippe Sylvain, "Les debuts du *Courrier du Canada* et le progrès de l'ultramontanisme canadien-français." *Cahiers de Dix* 32 1967 255-77.

379   Philippe Sylvain, "Libéralisme et ultramontanisme au Canada-français: affrontement idéologique et doctrinal (1840-1865)." *The shield of Achilles/Le bouclier d'Achille*. Ed. par W.L. Morton. Toronto: McClelland and Stewart, 1968. 111-38, 220-55.

380   Guy Sylvestre, *Panorama des lettres canadiennes françaises*. Québec: Ministère des Affaires Culturelles, 1964. 82p. Bibliographie, p.77.

381   T.H.B. Symons, *To know ourselves*. Report of the Commission on Canadian Studies. By T.H.B. Symons *et al*. Association of Universities and Colleges of Canada, 1975.   2 vols.   Section on philosophy curriculum, p.99-102, notes p.138.

382   Cyprien Tanguay, *Répertoire général du clergé canadien par ordre alphabétique depuis la fondation de la colonie jusqu'à nos jours*. Québec: C. Darreau, 1868. 321, xxix, p. 2e ed. Montréal: Senecal et fils, 1893. xiii, 526, xliv p.

383   Robert Taylor, *The Darwinian revolution: the responses of four Canadian scholars*. Hamilton: 1976. Ph.D. dissertation, McMaster University. Examines the thought of William Dawson, Daniel Wilson, John Watson and Nathanael Burwash.

384   Terry J. Tekippe, *Lonergan bibliography: primary sources*. Edited by Terry J. Tekippe and Michael O'Callaghan. Computer print-out on request to editors of the *Lonergan Newsletter*. Copies in the library of St. Michael's College, Toronto and in the offices of the Bibliography of Philosophy in Canada. Includes all sorts of non-print materials as well as published works. Also provides analysis and some annotations about the works of the noted Jesuit philosopher and theologian.

385   Jean Tétreau, *Hertel, l'homme et l'oeuvre*. Montréal: Cercle du Livre de France, 1986. 339p. c.r.: *Liberté* 169 FE1987 100-4 (Réjean Beaudoin).

386   Claude Thibault, *Bibliographia Canadiana*. Don Mills: Longman, 1973. lxvi, 795p. A bibliographical guide to writings in Canadian history.

387   Pierre Thibault, "L'histoire du Thomisme québécois, ou de l'importance de mettre les âmes à leur place." *Philosophiques* 8/2 OC1981 343-8. Intervention sur Yvan Lamonde, *Philosophie et son enseignement au Québec 1665- 1920* (no. 220).

388   Pierre Thibault, *Savoir et pouvoir. Philosophie thomiste et politique cléricale au XIXe siècle*. Québec: Presses de l'Université Laval, 1972. xxviii, 252p. (Histoire et sociologie de la culture, no. 2.) c.r.: *Dialogue* 12/3 1973 552-5 (Léonce Pâquet).

389   Elizabeth Trott, *"The faces of reason* and its critics," by Elizabeth Trott and Leslie Armour. *Dialogue* 25/1 Spring 1986 105-18. A detailed response to a number of critical notices (including no. 132) of *The faces of reason* (no. 8).

390   Marcel Trudel, *L'influence de Voltaire au Canada.* Montréal: Fides, 1945. (Collection "L'Hermine") 2 vols: vol. 1, 1769-1850; vol. 2, 1850-1900. Bibliographie: vol. 2 p.259-311.

391   André Vidricaire, *Matériaux pour l'histoire des institutions universitaires de philosophie au Québec.* par André Vidricaire *et al.* Québec: Université Laval, Institut Superieur des Sciences Humaines, 1976. 2 vols. (Cahiers de l'Institut Superieur des Sciences Humaines, no. 4 t.1-2). Contient des descriptions historiques & bibliographies des départements et facultés de la philosophie au Québec depuis 1940.

392   Robert Vigneault, "De la philosophie comme écriture." *Lettres Québécoises* 42 Eté 1986 62-4. Commentaire sur l'écriture de Jean Theau.

393   Robert Charles Wallace, "Philosophy in Canadian education." *Culture* 2/4 DC1941 424-5.

394   Robert Charles Wallace, *Some great men of Queen's.* Ed. R.C. Wallace. Toronto: Ryerson, 1941. 133p. Includes biographies of John Watson and George Monro Grant, among others.

395   William Stewart Wallace, *A history of the University of Toronto, 1827-1927.* Toronto: University of Toronto Press, 1927. 308p. Deals mainly with institutional history.

396   Edward J. Walsh, *Philosophy and the history of ideas; dissertations in progress, Canada and the United States.* Lakewood, N.J.: Georgian Court College, 1970-. Annual. 1970 issue has title *Dissertations in progress: philosophy and the history of ideas.*

397   Douglas N. Walton, *Canadian developments in biomedical ethics of death and dying.* Unpublished, 26p. Bibliographical references. Available, office of Bibliography of Philosophy in Canada, Department of Philosophy, University of Toronto. Surveys Canadian legal definitions of death and Canadian philosophical writing on death and dying to end of 1978.

398   Jane Ward, "Published works of H.A. Innis: bibliography." *Canadian Journal of Economics and Political Science.* 19 MA 1953 233-44.

399   J.R. Watts, "George Monro Grant." *Some great men of Queen's.* Ed. R.C. Wallace, Toronto: Ryerson, 1941. 1- 21.

400 Joseph Watzlawik, *Leo XIII and the new scholasticism*. Cebu City (Phillipines): University of San Carlos Press, 1966. xvi, 225p. Includes a discussion of the early development of Thomism in Quebec and of its differences from American Thomism. p.71-2; cf. 67-71 on the United States.

401 Peter Weinrich, *Social protest from the left in Canada 1870-1970. A bibliography*. Toronto & Buffalo: University of Toronto Press, 1982. 627p. Includes indexes. Includes references to items of social criticism some of which have a philosophic content.

402 Michael Weinstein, *Culture critique; Fernand Dumont and new Quebec sociology*. New York: St. Martin's Press, 1985. 124p. Bibliographic notes 117-23. "Key readings" 124.

403 J.F. Willard, *Progress of medieval studies in the United States of America and Canada*. Bulletin no. 12. Boulder, Colorado: Medieval Academy of America and University of Colorado, 1935.

404 Edmund Wilson, *O Canada: an American's notes on Canadian culture*. New York: Octagon Books, 1976. c1965: Farrar, Strauss & Giroux.

405 Clifford John Williams, *The course of academic social philosophy in Canada 1850-1950*. Typescript. Sept. 1961. Identifies and describes major figures in the field. Available, office of Bibliography of Philosophy in Canada, Department of Philosophy, University of Toronto.

406 Clifford John Williams, *The epistemology of John Watson*. Toronto: 1966. Ph.D. thesis, University of Toronto, 330 l. Bibliography, 321-30.

407 Martha E. Williams, *Computer readable bibliographic data bases: a directory and data sourcebook*. By Martha E. Williams and Sandra H. Rouse. Washington: American Society for Information Science, 1976.

408 Jerzy A. Wojciechowski, *Survey on the status of philosophy in Canada/Enquête sur la situation de la philosophie au Canada*. Ottawa: Canadian Philosophical Association/L'Association Canadienne de Philosophie, 1970. A study of philosophy departments based on questionnaires to heads and members. It is extremely tabular in format and has unusual pagination. The results have been interpreted in no. 89.

409 Julian Wolfe, *Canadian philosophy books 1970-80 Livres de philosophie canadiens: 1970-80*. Ottawa: Carleton University, 1980. Compiled from lists supplied by heads of philosophy departments. There is also an expanded version of the English-language list, 1980.

410   Ellen Wood, *Thoughts on the present and the future of Canadian political science.* By Ellen & Neal Wood. Presented under the auspices of the University League for Social Reform, 29MR1969. 55p. Typescript. On the Americanization of Canadian universities. Available, office of the Bibliography of Philosophy in Canada, Department of Philosophy, University of Toronto.

Addenda 1989

411   Gilles Bibeau, "La contribution de Sapir à l'étude du langage." *La Petite Revue de Philosophie* 7/2 Printemps 1986 5-16. Cfr. nos. 415, 416, 426.

412   Alain Cadet, "Les "lectures" d'Etienne Parent: une lecture." *La Petite Revue de Philosophie* 8/1 Automne 1986 125-41.

413   Marc Chabot, "Les philosophes à la triste figure." *La Petite Revue de Philosophie* 8/1 Automne 1986 1-22. Sur la confrontation Louis-Antoine Dessaules/Alexis Pelletier.

414   Yvan Cloutièr, "Philosophie et marketing: Sortre à Montréal, mars 1946." *Philosophiques* 15/1 Printemps 1988 169-90.

415   Ian Drummond, *Political economy at the University of Toronto: a history of the department, 1888-1982.* Toronto: Faculty of Arts & Science, 1983. 189p. Appendix I: Members of the Department's Academic Staff, 1888-1982 p.166-73. Appendix II: Ph.D.'s Conferred, p. 174-89. The department has contained a number of important contributors to political and social philosophy.

416   David Fielding, "L'hypothèse Sapir." *La Petite Revue de Philosophie* 7/2 Printemps 1986 17-46. Cfr. nos. 411, 417, 428.

417   Claude Gagnon, "Commentaires sur les contributions de Gilles Bibeau et de David Fielding." *La Petite Revue de Philosophie* 6/2 Printemps 1985 47-55. Cfr. nos. 411, 416, 428.

418   Christine Gohier, "Femme et philosophie au Québec." *La Petite revue de Philosophie* 6/2 Printemps 1985 83-93.

419   Tory Hoff, *The controversial appointment of James Mark Baldwin to the University of Toronto in 1889.* Ottawa: 1980. M.A. Thesis Carleton University. On the dispute between partisans of Baldwin and partisans of James Gibson Hume to fill the chair vacated on the death of G. Paxton Young.

420   Roland Houde, "Dominique-Ceslas Gonthier, o.p. 1853-1917; perception et réception." *La Petite Revue de Philosophie* 8/1 Automne 1986 189-214.

421   Susan E. Houston, *Schooling and Scholars in Nineteenth-Century Ontario*. By Susan E. Houston & Alison Prentice. Toronto: University of Toronto Press, 1988. xiv, 418p. (Ontario Historical Studies Series) Includes discussion of educational ideologies and of the role of George Paxton Young as grammar school inspector.

422   Yvan Lamonde, "Le destin de Descartes au Québec (1665-1920) et la tradition philosophique occidentale." *La Petite Revue de Philosophie* 8/2 Printemps 1987 151-8

423   Maurice Langlois, "Foi et raison chez T.-A. Chandonnet (le problème d'une traversée)." *La Petite Revue de Philosophie* 8/1 Automne 1986 143-60.

424   Danielle Leclerc, "Une trace allemande insoupçonnée au coeur de notre XIX siècle." *La Petite Revue de Philosophie* 8/1 Automne 1986 103-24. Sur l'influence de Hegel, par l'intermédiare, Victor Cousin, sur Louis-Antoine Dessaules.

425   A. Brian McKillop, *Contours of Canadian Thought*. Toronto: University of Toronto Press, 1987. 163p. Bibliographical notes, p.129-54. Essays on Canadian intellectual history in the 19th and early 20th centuries, with 3 chapters (1-3) on the writing of intellectual history. Ch.7 previously appeared as no. 260.

426   Harel Malouin, "Le libéralisme: 1848-1851." *La Petite Revue de Philosophie* 8/1 Automne 1986 59-101. Sur Louis-Antoine Dessaules et la pensée libérale au Québec.

427   Michael L. Morgan, *The Jewish thought of Emil Fackenheim, a reader*. Ed. & introd. Michael L. Morgan. Selected in collaboration with Emil L. Fackenheim. Detroit: Wayne State University Press, 1987. 394p. Bibliography of works by Emil Fackenheim, p.381-8. A reader of selections from talks, essays and books on Jewish topics. Includes a first publication and English translation of "Unsere Stellung zur Halacha" (1938).

428   Robert Nadeau, "Présentation," aux articles sur l'héritage d'Edward Sapir (1884-1939). *La Petite Revue de Philosophie* 7/2 Printemps 1986 3-4. Cfr. nos. 411, 416, 417.

429   Morton Paterson, *Divine encounter in Blewett*. Paper presented at the annual meeting of the Canadian Society for the Study of Religion, Edmonton, 1975. Typescript, 17p. Available, office of the Bibliography of Philosophy in Canada, Department of Philosophy, University of Toronto.

430   Morton Paterson, *G.J. Blewett: a link between Würzburg and personalism*. 15OC1975. Typescript, 7p. Available, office of the Bibliography of Philosophy in Canada, Department of Philosophy, University of Toronto.

431   Claude-Elizabeth Perreault, "Paul-Marc Sauvalle, un journaliste rebelle." *La Petite Revue de Philosophie* 8/1 Automne 1986 161-87.

432   Michael Pomedli, "Beyond unbelief; early Jesuit interpretations of native religions." *Studies in Religion/Sciences Religieuses* 16/3 Summer 1987 275-87.   On attempts of early Jesuit missionaries to Canada to interpret the belief system of native people.

433   John Douglas Rabb, "Herbert L. Stewart, Thomas Carlyle and Canadian idealism." *Canadian Literature* 111 1986 211-4.

434   John Douglas Rabb, *Religion and Science in early Canada*. Edited by J. Douglas Rabb. Kingston: Ronald P. Frye & Company, 1988. ix, 438p. Discussion of and texts by John Watson, J.C. Murray, James Beaven, William Lyall, George Paxton Young, William A. Crawford-Frost, Jacob Gould Schurman, G.J. Blewett, H.C. Stewart and others.

435 Rainer Raehre, *The psychiatric theory of Richard M. Bucke: a study in the impact of evolutionary naturalism on psychiatric thought in late-Victorian Canada*. Presented at the meetings of the Canadian Society for the History and Philosophy of Science. Saskatoon 4JN1979. Typescript, 48p. Available, office of the Bibliography of Philosophy in Canada, Department of Philosophy, University of Toronto.

436 Marlene Shore, *The Science of social redemption; McGill, the Chicago school and the origins of social research in Canada*. Toronto: University of Toronto Press, 1987, xviii, 340p. Includes discussion of the philosophers' attitudes towards it.

437   S.E.D. Shortt, *Victorian Lunacy: Richard M. Bucke and the practice of Late -Nineteenth Century psychiatry*. New York: Cambridge U. Press, 1986. 207p. c.r. *Canadian Historical Review* 68/4 DC1987 663-4 (Angus McLaren).

438   Richard W. Vaudry, "Theology and education in early Victorian Canada: Knox College, Toronto, 1844-61." *Studies in Religion/Sciences Religieuses* 16/4 Fall 1987 431-47. Discusses the role of philosophical training in theological education at Knox and the work there of Henry Esson and George Paxton Young.

439   Beatrice Anne Wood, *Idealism transformed; the making of a progressive educator*. Kingston: McGill-Queen's University Press, 1985. xiv, 232p. Bibliographical references.   On John Harold Putnam (1866-1940) an Ottawa educator influenced by Canadian idealist philosophy.

440   Suzanne Zeller, *Inventing Canada; early Victorian Science and the ideal of a transcontinental nation*. Toronto: University of Toronto Press, 1987. vi, 356p. Includes discussion of 19th century debates over taxonomic principles in biology.

Part III/Troisième Partie

Some Important Published Works by Early English Canadian Philosophers

Quelques publications d'importance par certains proto-philosophes anglo-canadiens

Beattie, Francis Robert 1848-1906

A1   *Apologetics; or the rational vindication of Christianity.* Richmond, Va.: Presbyterian Committee of Publications, 1903. 605p.

A2   *Calvinism and modern thought.* Philadelphia: Westminster Press, 1901. 48p.

A3   *An examination of the utilitarian theory of morals.* Brantford: J. & J. Sutherland Publishers, 1885. 222p.

A4   *The higher criticism;or modern critical theories as to the origin and contents of the literature and religion found in the holy scriptures.* Toronto: William Briggs, 1888. Pamphlet.

A5   *The methods of theism; an essay.* Brantford: Watt, 1887. 138p.

Beaven, James 1801-75

A6   *An account of the life and writings of St. Irenaeus.* London: 1841.

A7   *De finibus malorum et bonorum. On the supreme good.* By Marcus Tullius Cicero. With a preface, English notes, etc., partly from Madvig and others by the Reverend James Beaven. London: T&J Rivington, 1853.

A8   *Elements of natural theology.* London: Rivington, 1850. 240p.

Blewett, George John 1873-1912

A9   *The Christian view of the world.* Toronto: William Briggs, & New Haven: Yale University Press, 1912. 344p. (Nathanael Taylor Lectures, 1910-12).

A10   Review of *Studies in mystical religion* by Rufus M. Jones. *Philosophical Review* 18/6 1910 663-6.

A11   *The study of nature and the vision of God: with other essays in philosophy.* Toronto: William Briggs, 1907. 358p. Includes essays on nature and the vision of God, Spinoza, Plato, Erigena, Thomas Aquinas, Idealism.

A12   "The scientist and the vision of God." *Acta Victoriana* 21 1898 316-26.

Bovell, James 1817-80

A13 *Outlines of natural theology, for the use of the Canadian student, selected and arranged from the most authentic sources.* Toronto: Rowsell & Ellis, 1859. 8p., 649p.

A14 *Passing thoughts on man's relation to God and on God's relation to man.* Toronto: Rowsell & Ellis 1862, xiv, 427p.

Brett, George Sydney 1879-1944

A15 "The achievement of Santayana." *University of Toronto Quarterly* 9/1 OC1939 22-37.

A16 "Aquinas, Hollywood and Freud." *Ethics* 49/2 JA1939 204-11. Review of two books by Mortimer Adler.

A17 "Arms and the nation." *University of Toronto Monthly* 16 FE1916 232-7.

A18 "Associationism and 'act' psychology: a historical retrospect." *Psychologies of 1930.* Ed. C. Murchison. Worcester, Mass.: Clark University Press, 1930. 39-55.

A19 "Astronomical symbolism." *Journal of the Royal Astronomical Society of Canada* 20 NO-DC1926 335-50.

A20 "Bishop Berkeley." *Royal Society of Canada, Transactions* 27/sect.2 1933 109-17.

A21 "The classifying mind." *University of Toronto Quarterly* 7 OC1937 131-5.

A22 "Concerning the common mind." *University of Toronto Monthly* 15 MR1915 243-8.

A23 "The dean and the astronomers." *University of Toronto Quarterly* 3 JA1934 251-7.

A24 "Democracy and education." *School* 6 OC1917 137-41.

A25 "The effect of the discovery of the barometer on modern thought." *Journal of the Royal Astronomical Society of Canada* 38 1944 7-20.

A26 "The emergence of Christianity." *University of Toronto Quarterly* 3 JL1934 537-40.

A27 "The evolution of orthodoxy." *Canadian Journal of Religious Thought* 3 AL1926 95-100.

A28   "From philosophy to theology." *Canadian Journal of Religious Thought* 7 SE-OC1930 320-4.

A29   "Goethe's place in the history of science." *University of Toronto Quarterly* 1/3 AL1932 279-99.

A30   *The government of man; an introduction to ethics and politics.* London: Bell, 1913. 318p.

A31   "Graduate studies, present and future." *University of Toronto Monthly* 20 FE1920 169-71.

A32   "Higher education." *Annals of the American Academy of Political and Social Sciences* 107 MA1923 126-30.

A33   *Historia de la psicologia.* Buenos Aires: Ediciones Paidós, 1963. 686p. Tr. and abr. of *A history of psychology.*

A34   "The historical development of the theory of emotions." *Feeling and emotions: the Wittenberg symposium.* Ed. M.L. Reymert. Worcester, Mass.: Clark University Press, 1928. p.388-97.

A35   *A history of psychology.* London: George Allen, 1912-21. 3 vols.: 388, 394, 322p. (Library of Philosophy, Ed. J.H. Muirhead).

A36   *History of psychology.* Revised edition. Ed. & abr. R.S. Peters. London: Allen & Unwin, & New York: Macmillan, 1955. 778p. Contains bibliography.

A37   *History of psychology.* 2nd rev. ed. Ed. & abr. R.S. Peters. Cambridge, Mass.: Massachusetts Institute of Technology, 1965. 778p.

A38   "The history of science as a factor in modern education." *Royal Society of Canada, Transactions* 19/sect.2 1925 39-46.

A39   "The intellectual aspect of the relations between India and the West." *Royal Society of Canada, Transactions* 25/sect.2 1931 109-16.

A40   "The interpretation of political theory." *Royal Society of Canada, Transactions.* 24/sect.2 1930 63-9.

A41   *Introduction to Psychology.* Toronto: Macmillan, 1929. 193p.

A42   "The limits of science." *University of Toronto Monthly* 14 NO1913 34-8.

A43   "Maimonides." *Royal Society of Canada, Transactions* 29/sect.2 1935 33-42.

A44 "Makers of science." *University of Toronto Quarterly* 5 JL1936 605-11.

A45 "The modern mind and modernism." *Canadian Journal of Religious Thought* 5 MR-AL1928 91-104.

A46 "Newton's place in the history of religious thought." *Sir Isaac Newton, 1727-1927.* Baltimore: 1928. (Special publication of the History of Science Society, no. 1). 257-73.

A47 "Parallel paths in philosophy and literature." *University Magazine* 18/1 AL1919 218-38.

A48 "Paul Elmer More: a study." *University of Toronto Quarterly* 4 AL1935 279-95.

A49 *The philosophy of Gassendi.* London: Macmillan, 1908. 310p.

A50 "Philosophy teaching in the University of Toronto." *Culture* 2/4 DC1941 434-5.

A51 "The present status of psychological science in different countries: Canada." *Scandinavian Scientific Review* 3 1924 208-15.

A52 "The problem of freedom after Aristotle." *Mind* N.S. no.87 JL1913 361-72.

A53 *Psychology, ancient and modern.* New York: Longmans, 1928. 164p. Includes bibliography. (Our Debt to Greece and Rome, ed. G.D. Hadzits & D.M. Robinson, no.48). Repr. 1963 New York: Cooper Square Publications.

A54 "Psychology, history of." *Encyclopaedia Britannica*, 14 ed. vol. 18. London & N.Y.: 1929. 706-20.

A55 "The psychology of William James in relation to philosophy." *In commemoration of William James, 1842-1942.* New York: Columbia University Press, 1942. 81-94.

A56 "The revolt against reason." *Royal Society of Canada, Transactions* 13/sect.2 1920 9-17.

A57 "Shelley's relation to Berkeley and Drummond." *Studies in English by members of University College, Toronto.* Ed. M.W. Wallace. Toronto: University of Toronto Press, 1931. 170-202.

A58 "The sociology of law." *University of Toronto Quarterly* 14 OC1944 105-7.

A59   "Some beliefs about psychology." *Canadian Journal of Religious Thought* 1 NO-DC1924 473-80.

A60   "Some reflections on Aristotle's theory of tragedy." *Philosophical essays presented to John Watson.* Kingston: Queen's University, 1922. 158-78.

A61   "Thomas Hill Green." *Encyclopaedia of religion and ethics.* Ed. J. Hastings. Edinburgh: T. & T. Clark, 1913. 435-40.

A62   "Transformation of belief--historical." *Knox College Alumni Association lectures.* Delivered at the annual conference, 1935. Toronto: Bloor Press for the Association, 1935. 1-19 (Lecture no.1).

A63   "William James and American ideals." *University of Toronto Quarterly* 6/2 JA1937 159-73.

A64   Review of *Chrysippe* by Emile Bréhier. *Philosophical Review* 20 SE1911 551-4.

A65   Review of *The mind and its place in nature* by C.D. Broad. *Philosophical Review* 37 MR1928 181-5.

A66   Review of *What Plato said* by Paul Shorey. *International Journal of Ethics* 44 OC1933 134-8.

Bucke, Richard Maurice 1837-1902

A67   *Cosmic consciousness, a study in the evolution of the human mind.* Philadelphia: Innes & Sons, 1901. 318p. Repr. 1905, 1923 (Dutton, 384p.), 1943 (Blakiston), 1946 (Dutton, with new introduction by George Acklom, 384p.), 1948, 1961 (University Books, 326p.), 1969 (Dutton), 1970 (Citadel 326p.), 1974 (Causeway).

A68   *Die Erfahrung des kosmischen Bewusstseins: eine Studie zur Evolution des menschlichen Geistes.* Uebersetzt von Karin Reise. Freiburg: Aurum Verlag, 1975. 216p. Tr. of *Cosmic consciousness.*

A69   "The growth of the intellect." *American Journal of Insanity* 39/1 JL1882 36-54.

A70   *Man's moral nature: an essay.* Toronto: Willing & Williamson, & New York: Putnam, 1879. 200p.

A71   "The moral nature and the great sympathetic." *American Journal of Insanity* 35/2 OC1878 229-53.

A72   "The origin of insanity." *American Journal of Insanity* 49/1 JL1892 56-66.

A73 "Insanity." *American Journal of Insanity* 47/1 JL1890 17-26.

Crawford, Alexander Wellington 1866-19?

A74 "Empiricism and metaphysics." *University of Toronto Quarterly* 2 JA1896 148-54.

Crawford-Frost, William Albert 1863-1936

A75 *A new theory of evolution.* College Park: University of Maryland, 1926. 22p. Contains "Science, philosophy and religion," & "From amoeba to American."

A76 *Old dogma in a new light.* New York: St. Mary's Publishing Guild, 1896. 56p.

A77 *The philosophy of integration; An explanation of the universe and of the Christian religion.* Ed. James Wilson Bright. Boston: Mayhew Publishing Co., 1906. 182p.

A78 *The way out.* 1931. 8p., accompanied by "Notes on *The way out.*" (Pamphlets on International Cooperation 2/2).

Dawson, Sir John William 1820-1899

A79 "Introduction of genera and species in geological time." *Canadian Monthly and National Review* 2 AU1872 154-6.

A80 *Modern ideas of evolution as related to revelation and science.* London: Religious Tract Society, 1890. 240p. Frequently reissued.

A81 Review of "Darwin on the origin of species by means of natural selection." *Canadian Naturalist and Geologist* 5 1860 100-20.

Dyde, Samuel Walters 1862-1947

A82 "Basis for ethics." *Mind* 13 1888 549-79.

A83 "Evolution and development." *Philosophical Review* 4 1895 1-21.

A84 "Hegel's conception of crime and punishment." *Philosophical Review* 7 1898 62-71.

A85 "Hegel's conception of freedom." *Philosophical Review* 3 1894 655-71.

A86 *Hegel's philosophy of right.* Tr. by S.W. Dyde. London: George Bell & Sons, 1896. xxx, 365p. Translator's preface p.ix-xiii.

A87   "Plato's style and method." *Queen's Quarterly* 5/3 1898 173-85.

A88   "Socrates, his person and work." *Queen's Quarterly* 11 1902 43-56.

A89   *The Theaetetus of Plato.* Tr. by S.W. Dyde. Kingston: Wm. Bailie Printer, 1890. 85p.

A90   *The Theaetetus of Plato.* Tr, with an introduction by S.W. Dyde. Glasgow: James Maclehose & Sons, 1899.

A91   Review of Bernard Bosanquet, *The philosophical theory of the state. Philosophical Review* 9 1900 198-206.

George, James 1801-1870

A92   *An address delivered at the opening of Queen's College, 1853.* Kingston: 1853.

A93   *An address delivered on the 5th of April, 1855, before the Senate and students of Queen's College, on conferring the degree of Doctor of Medicine.* Kingston: 1855. On the mind-body relationship.

A94   *The duties of subjects to their rulers, with a special view to the present time; a sermon preached in the Presbyterian Church of Scarborough.* Toronto: printed by W.J. Coates, 1838. 32p. Motto: "Pro rege, lege et grege."

A95   *The mission of Great Britain to the world or Some of the lessons which she is now teaching; a lecture delivered at Stratford...*Toronto: Dudley & Burns, 1867. 22p.

A96   *Moral courage, an address...opening of the 15th session of Queen's College* ....Kingston: Creighton, 1856.

A97   *The relation between piety and intellectual labour. An address delivered at the opening of the fourteenth session of Queen's College.* Kingston: Printed at the Daily News Office, 1855. 24p.

A98   *Thoughts on high themes, being a collection of sermons from the mss. of the late James George.* Toronto: Campbell, 1874. 262p.

A99   *The value of earnestness; an address delivered at the opening of the thirteenth session of the University of Queen's College.* Kingston: Printed at the Daily News Office, 1854. 16p.

A100   *What is civilization? A lecture delivered in the City Hall, with a view of aiding to raise the bursary fund.* Kingston: Creighton, 1859. 50p.

Keirstead, Wilfrid Currier 1871-1944

A101 "Essential facts of social progress." *Biblical World* 39 JA1912 38-46.

A102 "Ideals in dictatorships and democracies." *Dalhousie Review* 19 AL1939 41-8.

A103 "Metaphysical presuppositions of Ritschl." *American Journal of Theology* 9 1905 677-718. Based on a Ph.D. dissertation, U. of Chicago.

A104 "Philosophy, its data and its aims." *Culture* 2/4 DC1941 435-40.

A105 "Theological presuppositions of Ritschl." *American Journal of Theology* 10 JL1906 423-51.

LeSueur, William Dawson 1840-1917

A106 "The anarchy of modern politics." *Popular Science Monthly* 23 AU1883 444-53.

A107 "Carlyle and Comte." *Rose-Belford's Canadian Monthly* 6 JN1881 639-42.

A108 "Creation or evolution?" *Popular Science Monthly* 31 MA1887 29-39.

A109 *A defence of modern thought. In reply to a recent pamphlet by the Bishop of Ontario, on 'Agnosticism'.* Toronto: Hunter & Rose, 1884. 40p.

A110 "A defence of modern thought." *Popular Science Monthly* 24 AL1884 780-93. An abridged form of the pamphlet.

A111 "Education, past and present." *University of Toronto Monthly* 12 MA1911 279-92.

A112 "Evolution and the destiny of man." *Popular Science Monthly* 26 FE1885 456-68.

A113 *Evolution and the positive aspects of modern thought. In reply to the Bishop of Ontario's second lecture on Agnosticism.* Ottawa: A.S. Woodbury, 1884. 43p.

A114 "Evolution bounded by theology." *Popular Science Monthly* 29 JN1886 145-53.

A115 "Ex-president Porter on evolution." *Popular Science Monthly* 29 SE1886 577-94.

A116   "A few words on criticism." *Rose-Belford's Canadian Monthly* 3 SE1879 323-8.

A117   "Free thought and responsible thought." *Rose-Belford's Canadian Monthly* 8 JN1882 614-20.

A118   "The future of morality." *Rose-Belford's Canadian Monthly* 4 JA1880 74-82.

A119   "History, its nature and methods." *Royal Society of Canada, Transactions* 3 series 7 Appendix A 1913 lvii-lxxxiii. Presidential Address to the Royal Society.

A120   "Idealism in life." *Canadian Monthly and National Review* 13/4 AL1878 414-20.

A121   "The intellectual life." *Canadian Monthly and National Review* 7 AL1875 320-30.

A122   "Kidd on social evolution." *Popular Science Monthly* 47 MA1895 38-48.

A123   "Liberty of thought and discussion." *Canadian Monthly and National Review* 10/3 SE1876 202-12.

A124   "Materialism and positivism." *Popular Science Monthly* 20 MR1882 615-21.

A125   "Messrs. Moody and Sankey and revivalism." *Canadian Monthly and National Review* 7 JN1875 510-3.

A126   "Mr. Goldwin Smith on 'The data of ethics'." *Popular Science Monthly* 22 DC1882 145-56.

A127   "Mr. Mallock on optimism." *Popular Science Monthly* 35 AU1889 531-41.

A128   "Mr. Spencer and his critics." *Rose-Belford's Canadian Monthly* 4 AL1880 413-22. Repr. as "A vindication of scientific ethics."

A129   "Modern culture and Christianity," by Laon (pseud.). *Canadian Monthly and National Review* 8 DC1875 523-33.

A130   "The moral nature and intellectual power." *Rose-Belford's Canadian Monthly* 3 JL1879 104-5.

A131   "Morality and religion." *Rose-Belford's Canadian Monthly* 4 FE1880 166-71.

A132 "Morality and religion again, a word with my critics." *Rose-Belford's Canadian Monthly* 4 JN1880 642-55.

A133 "Morality without theology." *Rose-Belford's Canadian Monthly* 5 NO1880 522-8.

A134 "Notes on the study of language." *Transactions of the Ottawa Literary and Scientific Society* 9FE1900 93-118.

A135 "Physics and metaphysics." *Rose-Belford's Canadian Monthly* 8 AL1882 352-60. Reprinted as "Stallo's 'Concepts of modern physics'," *Popular Science Monthly.*

A136 "Prayer and modern thought." *Canadian Monthly and National Review* 8/2 AU1875 145-55.

A137 "Prayer and natural law." *Canadian Monthly and National Review* 9 MR1876 211-21.

A138 "The problem of popular government." *University of Toronto Monthly* 1 AL1901 229-41 & MA1901 257-63.

A139 *The problem of popular government. A lecture delivered in the Chemical Building, University of Toronto, February 23, 1901.* Toronto: 1901. 18p.

A140 "'Progress and poverty' and the doctrine of evolution." *Rose-Belford's Canadian Monthly* 6 MR1881 287-96.

A141 "Proofs and disproofs," by Laon (pseud.). *Canadian Monthly and National Review* 8 OC1875 339-48.

A142 "Ste.-Beuve." *Westminster Review* 95 1871 208-27.

A143 "Science and its accusers." *Popular Science Monthly* 34 JA1889 367-79.

A144 "Science and materialism." *Canadian Monthly and National Review* 11 JA1877 22-8.

A145 "The scientific spirit." *Rose-Belford's Canadian Monthly* 3 DC1879 437-41.

A146 "Stallo's 'Concepts of modern physics'." *Popular Science Monthly* 21 MA1882 96-100.

A147 "A vindication of scientific ethics." *Popular Science Monthly* 17 JL1880 324-37.

A148 "War and civilization." *Popular Science Monthly* 48 AL1896 758-71.

Lighthall, William Douw 1857-1954

A149 *The altruistic act; an essay in ethics*, by Alchemist. Montreal: 1884. 12p.

A150 *An analysis of the altruistic act in illustration of a general outline of ethics.* Montreal: 1885. 20p.

A151 *The cosmic aspect of outer consciousness.* Montreal: author, 1924. 16p.

A152 "The directive power." *Philosophical Review* 37/6 NO1928 600-6.

A153 *An essay on pure ethics, with a theory of the motive.* Montreal: 1882. 15p.

A154 "The knowledge that is in instinct." *Philosophical Review* 39/5 SE1930 491-501.

A155 "The law of cosmic evolutionary adaptation." *Royal Society of Canada, Transactions* 34/sect.2 1940 135-41.

A156 "An organic superpersonality? a rejoinder." *Philosophical Review* 36/4 JL1927 372-3.

A157 *The outer consciousness.* Montreal: the author, 1923. 8p.

A158 *The outer consciousness in ethics.* Montreal: the author, 1924.

A159 *The outer consciousness and a future life.* Montreal: the author, 1925. 22p.

A160 "The permanence of Christianity." *Rose-Belford's Canadian Monthly* 8 MA1882 525-30.

A161 *The person of evolution: the outer consciousness, the outer knowledge, the directive power, studies of instinct as contribution to a philosophy of evolution.* Montreal: Kennedy, 1930. 216p.

A162 *The person of evolution.* Enlarged ed. Toronto: Macmillan, 1933. 246p.

A163 *The person of the outer consciousness.* Montreal: 1924.

A164 *A philosophy of purpose.* Montreal: the author, 1920. 15p.

A165 *Sketch of a new utilitarianism, including a criticism of the ordinary argument from design, and other matters.* Montreal: Witness, 1887. 40p.

A166 *Spiritualized happiness-theory; or new utilitarianism. A lecture before the Farmington School of Philosophy.* Montreal: Witness, 1890. 22p.

A167 *Superpersonalism: the outer consciousness a biological entity.* Montreal: Witness, 1926. 115p.

A168 *The teleology of the outer consciousness.* Montreal: Author, 1924. 13p.

Lodge, Rupert Clendon 1886-1961

A169 "The anatomy of humour." *Queen's Quarterly* 43 1936 55-61.

A170 *Applied philosophy.* London: Routledge & Kegan Paul, & Boston: Beacon, 1951. xi, 242p.

A171 "Balanced philosophy and eclecticism." *Journal of Philosophy* 41/4 17FE1944 85-91.

A172 "Bosanquet and the future of logic." *Philosophical Review* 32/6 NO1923 589-98.

A173 "Comments II." *Philosophy in Canada, a symposium.* Ed. John Irving. Toronto: University of Toronto Press, 1952. 44-8.

A174 "The comparative method in philosophy." *Manitoba essays.* Ed. Rupert Clendon Lodge. Toronto: Macmillan of Canada, 1937. 403-32.

A175 "Comparative philosophy." *Philosophic Mind* 2/2 1940 2-3.

A176 "De amicitia." *International Journal of Ethics* 47/2 JA1937 224-30.

A177 "The division of judgments." *Journal of Philosophy* 15 1918 541-50.

A178 "Empiricism." *Hasting's encyclopaedia of religion and ethics*, vol. 5. Edinburgh: Clark, 1912. 295-6.

A179 "The genesis of moral judgment in Plato." *International Journal of Ethics* 33 OC1922 34-54.

A180 *The great problems,* by Bernardino Varisco. Ed. & tr. from the Italian by Rupert Clendon Lodge. London: George Allen, 1914. xi, 370p. ("Library of Philosophy," ed. by J.H. Muirhead).

A181 *The great thinkers.* London: Routledge & Kegan Paul, 1949. x, 310p. (International Library of Philosophy). First American ed.: Boston: Beacon, 1951. Repr. New York: Ungar, 1964; New York: Kennikat, 1968.

A182 "Idealistic logic and philosophical construction." *Philosophical Review* 41 MA1932 300-11.

A183 "Immortality in recent philosophy." *Queen's Quarterly* 42/2 Summer 1935 234-41.

A184 *An introduction to modern logic*. Minneapolis: Perine Book Co., 1920. xiv, 361p.

A185 "The logical status of elementary and reflective judgments." *Journal of Philosophy* 17 1920 214-20.

A186 *Manitoba essays, written in commemoration of the sixtieth anniversary of Manitoba by members of the teaching staff of the university and of its affiliated colleges*. Ed. Rupert Clendon Lodge. Toronto: Macmillan of Canada, 1937. xiii, 342p.

A187 *The meaning and function of simple modes in the philosophy of John Locke*. Minneapolis: University of Minnesota Press, 1918. vi, 86p. Includes bibliography (U. of Minnesota: Studies in the Social Sciences). Published version of author's Ph.D. dissertation, U. of Minnesota.

A188 "Mind in Platonism." *Philosophical Review* 35 MA1926 201-20.

A189 "Modern logic and the elementary judgment." *Journal of Philosophy* 18 1921 42-8.

A190 *Modern logic and the problem of life; an inaugural lecture delivered by R.C. Lodge of the Department of Philosophy*. Winnipeg: University of Manitoba, 1921. 11p.

A191 "Moral validity: a study in Platonism." *Philosophical essays presented to John Watson*. Kingston: Queen's University, 1922. 63-114.

A192 "Negation in traditional and modern logic." *Mind* N.S.29 1920 82-90.

A193 "On a recent hypothesis concerning the Platonic Socrates." *Proceedings of the Sixth International Congress of Philosophy, Harvard, 1926.* New York: Longman, Green & Co., 1927. 559-71.

A194 "Philosophy and education." *Dalhousie Review* 14/3 1935 281-90.

A195 "Philosophy and education." *The Philosopher* (London, Eng.) 14 1936 10-5.

A196 "Philosophy as taught in the University of Manitoba." *Culture* 2/4 DC1941 430-4.

A197 *Philosophy of business*. Chicago: University of Chicago Press, & London: Cambridge University Press, 1945. xiv, 432p.

A198 *Philosophy of education*. New York & London: Harper, 1937. x, 328p.

A199 *Philosophy of education.* Rev. ed. New York: Harper, 1947. x, 350p. Bibliography, p.342-6.

A200 "Philosophy of make-believe." *Manitoba Arts Review* Fall 1938 33-6.

A201 *The philosophy of Plato.* London: Routledge & Kegan Paul, & New York: Humanities, 1956. ix, 347p. Bibliography, p.333-5. (International Library of Psychology, Philosophy and Scientific Method).

A202 "Plato and freedom." *Royal Society of Canada, Transactions* 38 series 3/sect.2 1949 87-101.

A203 "Plato and progress." *Philosophical Review* 55 NO1946 651-67.

A204 "Plato and the judge of conduct." *International Journal of Ethics* 31 OC1920 51-65.

A205 "Plato and the moral standard." *International Journal of Ethics* 32 OC1921 21-39; JA1922 193-211.

A206 "Platonic happiness as an ethical ideal." *International Journal of Ethics* 36/3 AL1926 225-39.

A207 "The platonic highest good." *Philosophical Review* 36 SE1927 428-49; NO1927 535-51.

A208 "The platonic highest good--presidential address." *Proceedings and addresses of the American Philosophical Association* 1 1928 1-38.

A209 "Platonic immortality as the highest good." *International Journal of Ethics* 37 AL1927 288-306.

A210 "The Platonic value-scale." *International Journal of Ethics* 35/1 OC1924 1-23.

A211 "Plato's secret." *Dalhousie Review* 16/1 AL1936 35-40.

A212 *Plato's theory of art.* London: Routledge & Kegan Paul, & New York: Humanities, 1953. viii, 316p. (International Library of Psychology, Philosophy and Scientific Method). Repr. New York: Russell & Russell, 1975.

A213 *Plato's theory of education.* With an appendix on the education of women according to Plato by Solomon Frank. London: Kegan Paul, Trench & Trübner & New York: Harcourt, Brace, 1947. viii, 322p. (International Library of Psychology, Philosophy and Scientific Method). Repr. Harcourt, Brace, 1948; London: Routledge & Kegan Paul, 1950; New York: Russell & Russell, 1970.

A214   *Plato' theory of ethics; the moral criterion and the highest good.* London: Kegan Paul, Trench & Trübner, 1928. xiv, 558p. Bibliography, p.543-5. (International Library of Psychology, Philosophy and Scientific Method). Repr. 1950; Archon Books, 1966.

A215   "Power in Platonism." *Philosophical Review* 36 JA1927 22-43.

A216   "Private and public spirit in Platonism." *Philosophical Review* 34 JA1925 1-27.

A217   "The psychological aspect of the Platonic value-judgment." *Philosophical Review* 31 MA1922 237-56.

A218   *The questioning mind; a survey of philosophical tendencies.* London & Toronto: Dent, & New York: E.P. Dutton, 1937. 311p.

A219   *The questioning mind; a survey of philosophical tendencies.* Rev. ed. Winnipeg: University of Manitoba Press, 1947 vii, 312p.

A220   "Reality and the moral judgment in Plato." *Philosophical Review* 29 JL1920 355-73; SE1920 453-75.

A221   "Science and philosophy." *Question Mark* 8/1 1940 14-5, 30-1.

A222   "The self in modern thought." *University of Toronto Quarterly* 5/4 1936 583-604.

A223   "Soul, body, wealth, in Plato." *Philosophical Review* 32 SE1923 470-90; 33 JA1924 30-50.

A224   "Synthesis or comparison?" *Journal of Philosophy* 35 4AU1938 432-40.

A225   "Tests of truth." *Journal of Philosophy* 17 1920 71-7.

A226   "What Socrates knows." *Royal Society of Canada, Transactions* 45 series 3/sect.2 1951 19-34.

Logan, John Daniel 1869-1929

A227   *Aesthetic criticism in Canada; its aims, methods and status.* By Aloysius Novicius (pseud.). Toronto: McClelland, 1917. 29p.

A228   "The Aristotelian concept of *physis*." *Philosophical Review* 6/1 JA1897 18-42.

A229   "The Aristotelian teleology." *Philosophical Review* 6/4 1897 386-400.

A230 *Dalhousie University and Canadian literature, being the history of an attempt to have Canadian literature included in the curriculum of Dalhousie University. With a criticism and a justification.* Halifax: author, 1922. 24p.

A231 *Democracy, education and the new dispensation, a constructive essay in social theory....* Toronto: Briggs, 1908. 20p.

A232 "The postulates of a psychology of prose style; an essay read before the Western Philosophical Association at Lincoln, Nebraska, Jan. 2, 1901." *Education* DC1901 8p.

A233 *Psychology and the argument from design.* Boston: 1898.

A234 *The religious functions of comedy; a phase of the problem of evil treated from the point of view of Aristotle's Poetics and Metaphysics and of spiritual monism.* Toronto: Briggs, 1907. 18p.

A235 *Scott and Haliburton; an essay in the psychology of creative satiric humor.* Halifax: Allen, 1921. 22p.

A236 "Self-realization and the way out." *Monist* 19 OC1909 609-15.

A237 Review of *The sense of beauty* by George Santayana. *Philosophical Review* 6/2 MR1897 210-3.

Lyall, William 1811-1890

A238 "Addison." *Rose-Belford's Canadian Monthly* 2 AL1879 411-20.

A239 "Dr. Lyall's inaugural." *Dalhousie Gazette* 2 29NO1869 2-5.

A240 *Intellect, the emotions and man's moral nature.* Edinburgh: T. Constable & Co., 1855. 627p.

A241 *The philosophy of thought; a lecture delivered at the opening of the Free Church College, Halifax, Nova Scotia: Session 1852-3.* Halifax: Barnes, 1853. 14p.

A242 "Professor Lyall's address." *Dalhousie Gazette* 7 21NO1874 1-3, 7-8.

A243 "Remarks on metaphysics--Dr. Lyall." *Dalhousie Gazette* New Series 5 29AL1880 139-40.

A244 *Strictures on the idea of power, with special reference to the views of Dr. Brown, in his Inquiry into the relation of cause and effect.* Edinburgh: Johnstone, 1842. 52p.

A245 "Tennyson, a criticism." *Rose-Belford's Canadian Monthly* 1 OC1878 477-89.

A246   "Thomas Campbell, a criticism." *Rose-Belford's Canadian Monthly* 1 AU1878 187-97.

A247   "Wordsworth, a criticism." *Belford's Monthly Magazine* 3 AL1878 612-27.

MacEachran, John Malcolm 1878-1971

A248   "Crime and punishment." *The Press Bulletin* (U. of Alberta Extension) 17/6 MA1932 1-4.

A249   "John Watson, 1847-1939." *Some great men of Queen's*. Ed. R.C. Wallace. Toronto: Ryerson, 1941. 22-50.

A250   "A philosopher looks at mental hygiene." *Mental Hygiene* 16 JA1932 101-19.

A251   *Pragmatismus: eine neue Richtung der Philosophie*. Leipzig: Theodor Weicker, 1910. 86p.

A252   "Some present-day tendencies in philosophy." *Philosophical essays presented to John Watson*. Kingston: Queen's University, 1922. 275-97.

A253   "Twenty-five years of philosophical speculation." *These twenty-five years, a symposium*. Toronto: Macmillan of Canada, 1933. 79-113.

Machar, Agnes Maule 1837-1927

A254   "Buddha and Buddhism." *Canadian Monthly and National Review* 13 JA1878 164-71.

A255   "Buddhism and Christianity." *Canadian Monthly and National Review* 13 MA1878 509-20.

A256   "Charles Kingsley." *Canadian Monthly and National Review* 7 MR1875 249-53.

A257 "Compulsory education." *Rose-Belford's Canadian Monthly* 7 AU1881 174-8.

A258   "Creeds and confessions." *Canadian Monthly and National Review* 9 FE1876 134-46.

A259   "The divine law of prayer," by Fidelis. *Canadian Monthly and National Review* 10 AU1876 144-55.

A260   "A few words on university co-education," by Fidelis. *Rose-Belford's Canadian Monthly* 8 MR1882 313-9.

A261 "Higher education for women," by Fidelis. *Canadian Monthly and National Review* 7 FE1875 144-57.

A262 "Modern theology and modern thought," by Fidelis. *Rose-Belford's Canadian Monthly* 6 MR1881 297-304.

A263 "The new ideal of womanhood," by Fidelis. *Rose-Belford's Canadian Monthly* 2 JN1879 659-76.

A264 "Positivism versus Christianity," by Fidelis. *Rose-Belford's Canadian Monthly.* 6 MA1881 518-32.

A265 "Prayer and Christian belief," by Fidelis. *Canadian Monthly and National Review* 8 OC1875 328-34.

A266 "Prayer and modern doubt," by Fidelis. *Canadian Monthly and National Review* 8 SE1875 224-36. Response to W.D. LeSueur, no. A125.

A267 "Prayer for daily bread." *Canadian Monthly and National Review* 7 MA1875 415-25. On prayer and laws of nature.

A268 "A pressing problem," by Fidelis. *Rose-Belford's Canadian Monthly* 2 AL1879 455-69.

A269 "The seen and the unseen," by Fidelis. *Canadian Monthly and National Review* 9 JN1876 495-508.

A270 "The source of moral life," by Fidelis. *Rose-Belford's Canadian Monthly* 4 AL1880 343-51.

A271 "Woman's work," by Fidelis. *Rose-Belford's Canadian Monthly* 1 SE1878 295-311.

Murray, John Clark 1836-1917

A272 "An ancient pessimist." *Philosophical Review* 2 JA1893 24-34. On Hegesius the Cyrenaic.

A273 "Atomism and theism." *Canadian Monthly and National Review* 7 JA1875 31-9.

A274 "Can Canada be coerced into the Union?" *Open Court* 9 1895 4561.

A275 "Christian ethics." *Presbyterian College Journal* Mr1889.

A276 "Dreams." *New Dominion Monthly* 20 JN1877 481.

A277 "The dualistic conception of nature." *Monist* 6/3 AL1896 382-95.

A278 "The education of the will." *Educational Review* 2 JN1891 57-62.

A279 *Epimetheus, to my students.* Montreal: W.F. Brown, 1897. 12p.

A280 *A handbook of Christian ethics.* Edinburgh: T&T Clark, 1908. 328p.

A281 *A handbook of psychology.* London: Alexander Gardner, 1885. 422p.

A282 *A handbook of psychology.* 2ed. rev. London: Alexander Gardner, 1888. 435p. Also Boston: Cupples & Heard, 1889; Boston: DeWolfe & Fiske, 1890. 3ed. London: Gardner, 1890. 5ed. Boston: DeWolfe, Fiske & Co., & London: Gardner, 1897.

A283 *The higher education of women; an address at the opening of Queen's College at Kingston, 1871.* Kingston: 1871. 17p.

A284 "The idealism of Spinoza." *Philosophical Review* 5 1896 473-88.

A285 *The industrial kingdom of God.* Ed. from ms. by Leslie Armour & Elizabeth Trott. Ottawa: University of Ottawa Press, 1981. xxix, 144p. (Collection: Philosophica, vol. 18).

A286 *An introduction to ethics.* Boston: DeWolfe, Fiske, & Montreal: W.F. Brown, 1891. 407p.

A287 *An introduction to psychology; based on the author's Handbook of psychology.* Boston: Little Brown & Co., 1904. 517p. Repr. 1905.

A288 *Outline of Sir William Hamilton's philosophy. A textbook for students*, with an introduction by the Reverend James McCosh. Boston: Gould & Lincoln, & New York: Sheldon & Co., 1870. 257p. Repr. 1874, 1876.

A289 "Philosophy and the industrial life; a paper read at the Philosophical Congress, Chicago, August, 1893." *Monist* 4 1894 533-44.

A290 "Psychology in medicine." *Medical Journal* (Montreal) JN1892.

A291 "The revived study of Berkeley." *Macmillan's Magazine* 56 JL1887 161-73. Also *Living Age* 174 JL-SE1887 345-54.

A292 "The Roman Catholic Church and marriage." *Open Court* 18 331

A293 "Rousseau; his position in the history of philosophy." *Philosophical Review* 8 1899 357-70.

A294 "The Scottish philosophy." *Macmillan's Magazine* 39 DC1878 112-26. Review of James McCosh, *The Scottish philosophy, biographical, expository, critical.*

A295 "Sir William Hamilton." *Scottish Review* 8 JL1886 20-40.

A296 "Sir William Hamilton's philosophy: an exposition and criticism--I, the Scottish philosophy." *The Canadian Journal of Industry, Science and Art.* N.S.11/64 JA1867 207-24.

A297 "Sir William Hamilton's philosophy: an exposition and criticism--II, exposition of Hamilton's system." *The Canadian Journal....*N.S.11/65 SE1867 300-19.

A298 "Sir William Hamilton's philosophy: an exposition and criticism--III, criticism of Hamilton's system." *The Canadian Journal....*N.S.11/66 DC1867 367-88.

A299 "Sir William Hamilton's philosophy: an exposition and criticism--IV, criticism of Hamilton's system continued." *The Canadian Journal....*N.S.12/67 DC1868 57-85.

A300 "Solomon Maimon," *British Quarterly Review* 82 JL1885 77- .

A301 *Solomon Maimon: an autobiography.* Tr. from the German with additions and notes by John Clark Murray. London: Alexander Gardner, 1889. 307p.

A302 *The study of political philosophy.* The annual University Lecture in McGill College, Montreal, 1877. 18p.

A303 "A summer school of philosophy." *Scottish Review* 19 JA1892 98-113.

A304 *Thoughts on the higher education of women. The introductory lecture to the First Session of the Ladies Education Association of Montreal, Oct. 1871.* Montreal: 1871.

A305 *A vindication of theology.* Montreal: Dawson, 1877. 15p.

A306 "What should be the attitude of teachers of philosophy toward religion?" *International Journal of Ethics* 14 1904 353-62.

A307 Review of George John Blewett, *The study of nature and the vision of God. University of Toronto Monthly* 7 JN1907 202-5.

Nelles, Samuel Sobieski 1823-1887

A308 *Chapters in logic; containing Sir William Hamilton's lectures on modified logic and selections from the Port Royal logic.* Ed. with a preface by the Rev. S.S. Nelles. Texts from the Port Royal Logic tr. by T.S. Baynes. Toronto: Wesleyan Methodist Book Room, 1870. viii, 213p. Logic textbook for Victoria College.

Nicholson, Henry Alleyne 1844-1899

A309 "Man's place in nature." *Canadian Monthly and National Review* 1/1 JA1872 35-45. On Darwin.

A310 *On the bearing of certain palaeontological facts upon the Darwinian theory of the origin of species, and on the general doctrine of evolution....To which is added the discussion thereon.* London: Published for the Institute by R. Hardwicke, 1875. 34p. Repr. from the *Journal* of the transactions of the Victoria (Philosophical) Institute.

Ritchie, Eliza 1856-1933

A311 "Discussion--'The ethical implications of determinism' and response to comments by Julia Gulliver." *Philosophical Review* 3 1894 67-8.

A312 "Erasmus, a study in character." *Dalhousie Review* 6/2 1927 206-27.

A313 "The essential in religion." *Philosophical Review* 10/1 JA1901 1-11.

A314 "The ethical implications of determinism." *Philosophical Review* 2 1893 529-43.

A315 "Morality and the belief in the supernatural." *International Journal of Ethics* 7/2 1896 180-91.

A316 "Notes on Spinoza's conception of God." *Philosophical Review* 11/1 JA1902 1-15.

A317 "Pfleiderer on morality and religion." *Philosophical Review* 5/6 NO1896 619-23.

A318 *The problem of personality.* Ithaca, N.Y.: Andrus & Church, 1889. 42p. Published version of author's Ph.D. dissertation, Cornell University.

A319 "The reality of the finite in Spinoza's system." *Philosophical Review* 13/1 JA1904 16-29.

A320 "Reply" (to Norman Wilde on Ritchie on Pfleiderer). *Philosophical Review* 6/1 JA1897 67-8.

A321 "Spinoza." *Dalhousie Review* 12/3 1933 333-9.

A322 "The tolerance of error." *International Journal of Ethics* 14/2 1903 161-72.

A323 "Truth-seeking in matters of religion." *International Journal of Ethics* 11/1 1900 71-82.

Schurman, Jacob Gould 1854-1942 (U.S. citizen 1892-)

A324 "The adaptation of university work to the common life of the people." *N.Y. State Education Bulletin* 443 15MR1909.

A325 *Agnosticism and religion.* New York: C. Scribner's Sons, 1896. vii, 181p.

A326 *Belief in God: its origins, nature and basis, being the Winkley Lectures of the Andover Theological Seminary.* New York: Charles Scribner's Sons, 1890. x, 266p. Repr. 1892, 1893, 1896, 1902, 1907.

A327 *The centenary movement of thought, Commencement Address, Ohio State University.* 19JN1889. Columbus, Ohio: Ohio State University, 1889. 29p.

A328 *The ethical import of Darwinism.* New York: Charles Scribner's Sons, 1887. xv, 267p. Repr. 1888, 1897, 1903.

A329 *Jefferson and the public policies of today.* Charlottesville, Virginia: 1911. 19p. Repr. from the U. of Virginia Alumni Bulletin, July, 1911. "address delivered in Cabell Hall, April 13, 1911...."

A330 *Kantian ethics and the ethics of evolution, a critical study.* Published by Hibbert Trustees. London: Williams, & Edinburgh: Williams & Norgate, 1881. vi, 103p.

A331 "The manifest destiny of Canada." *Forum* MR1889 2-10.

Smith, Goldwin 1823-1910

A332 *Concerning doubt. A reply to "A clergyman," by a layman.* Oxford: J.L. Wheeler, 1861. 14p.

A333 *Does the Bible sanction American slavery?* Oxford & London: J. Henry & Parker, & Cambridge: Sever & Francis, 1863. 107p.

A334 *Guesses at the riddle of existence and other essays on kindred topics.* New York & London: Macmillan, 1897. ix, 244p. Repr. Freeport, N.Y.: Books for Libraries Press, 1972.

A335 *Essays on questions of the day, political and social.* Toronto: Copp Clark, & London: Macmillan, 1893. vii, 360p.

A336 "Has science found a new basis for morality and art?" *Popular Science Monthly* 20 1883 753- .

A337 "The immortality of the soul." *Canadian Monthly and National Review* 9 MA1876 408-16.

A338 *Labour and capital, a letter to a labour friend.* New York & London: Macmillan, 1907. v, 38p.

A339 *Lectures and essays.* New York: Macmillan, & Toronto: Hunter & Rose, 1881. viii, 336p.

A340 *Lectures on modern history, delivered in Oxford 1859-61.* Oxford & London: J.H. & J. Parker, 1861. 2, 40, 91p., 1l., 47, 32p. 2ed., 1865 190p. "Authorized Canadian edition," Toronto: Adam, Stevenson & Co., 1873. Repr. of 1ed.: Freeport, N.Y.: Books for Libraries, 1972.

A341 *On some supposed consequences of the doctrine of historical progress.* Oxford & London: J.H. & J. Parker, 1861. 47p.

A342 "The prospect of a moral interregnum." *Rose-Belford's Canadian Monthly* 3 DC1879 651-63. Revised version of an article which appeared slightly earlier in *Atlantic Monthly.*

A343 *Rational religion, and the rationalistic objections of the Brampton lectures for 1858.* Oxford: J.C. Wheeler, & London: Whittaker & Co., 1861. xiii, 146p.

A344 *The study of history: a lecture, June 1859.* Oxford: Parker, 1859. 35p. Repr. 1861, with postscripts.

Stewart, Herbert Leslie 1882-1953

A345 "The alleged egoism in the demand for personal immortality." *The Biblical World* 51/1 JA1918 19-30.

A346 "The alleged Prussianism of Thomas Carlyle." *International Journal of Ethics* 28 JA1918 159-78.

A347 "Anatole France and modernist Catholicism." *American Journal of Theology* 24/1 JA1920 30-45.

A348 *Anatole France, the Parisian.* New York & Toronto: Dodd, Mead, 1927. xiv, 394p. "Bibliography of Anatole France's chief works," p.385-6. Repr. Freeport, N.Y.: Books for Libraries Press, 1972.

A349 "The business morals of the middle class--what do they owe to the Reformation?" *Hibbert Journal* 40 JA1942 156-65.

A350 "Can parliamentary government endure?" *Hibbert Journal* 33 AL1935 343-56.

A351 "Canada in satire," by "an Anglo-Canadian." *Dalhousie Review* 3 1923 17-24. On C.W. Stanley, "Spiritual conditions in Canada."

A352 "Carlyle's conception of history." *Political Science Quarterly* 32/4 DC1917 570-89.

A353 "Carlyle's conception of religion." *American Journal of Theology* 21/1 JA1917 43-57.

A354 "Carlyle's place in philosophy." *Monist* 29 AL1919 1-28.

A355 "The Cartesian tercentenary: Descartes and his age." *Royal Society of Canada, Transactions* Third series 31/sect.2 1937 1-11.

A356 "The censorship of moving pictures," by "a censor." *Dalhousie Review* 1 AL1921 37-46.

A357 "The centenary of Renan." *Dalhousie Review* 3 OC1923 362-75.

A358 *A century of Anglo-Catholicism*. London & Toronto: J.M. Dent & Sons, & New York: Oxford University Press, 1929. xvii, 404p.

A359 "The challenge to moral conventions." *Dalhousie Review* 11/1 1931 99-113.

A360 "Criticism and Morality." *University Magazine* 18/3 OC1919 359-72.

A361 "Dante and the schoolmen." *Journal of the History of Ideas* 10/3 JA1949 357-73.

A362 "The declining fame of Thomas Carlyle." *Royal Society of Canada, Transactions* 14/sect.2 1920 11-29.

A363 "'Democratic' transformation of the university." *Culture* 11 JN1950 133-42.

A364 "The ethics of luxury and leisure." *American Journal of Sociology* 24/3 NO1918 241-59.

A365 "Euthanasia." *International Journal of Ethics* 29 OC1918 48-62.

A366 "Francis Bacon, a tercentenary." *Dalhousie Review* 6/3 1927 374-83.

A367 *From a library window; reflections of a radio commentator*. Toronto: Macmillan, 1940. viii, 323p.

A368 "The future of universities." *Dalhousie Review* 24 JL1944 207-18.

A369 "The great secularist experiment." *Hibbert Journal* 42 JA1944 107-15.

A370 "Hobbes and his England." *Queen's Quarterly* 57/4 Winter 1951 510-9.

A371 "Is patriotism immoral?" *American Journal of Sociology* 22/5 MR1917 616-29.

A372 "J.S. Mill's *Logic*, a post-centenary appraisal." *University of Toronto Quarterly* 17/4 JL1948 361-71.

A373 "James Anthony Froude and Anglo-Catholicism." *American Journal of Theology* 22/2 AL1918 253-73.

A374 "Jeremy Bentham; a centenary retrospect." *Dalhousie Review* 12/2 JL1932 231-47.

A375 "Law as a portal to philosophy." *Canadian Bar Review* FE1949 189-95.

A376 "Laying the blame on labour." *University of Toronto Quarterly* 15/4 JL1946 333-45.

A377 "Literature and learning five centuries ago." *Queen's Quarterly* 48/1 Spring 1941 17-28.

A378 "Lord Bryce's estimate of Canada." *Dalhousie Review* 1 JL1921 170-81.

A379 "Lord Morley's relation to history, to theology and to the churches." *American Journal of Theology* 23/2 AL1919 165-88.

A380 "Machiavelli and fascism." *University of Toronto Quarterly* 6/1 OC1936 33-48.

A381 "Machiavelli and history." *Queen's Quarterly* 55/3 Autumn 1948 270-81.

A382 "Machiavelli and twofold truth." *Personalist* 19/2 Spring 1938 187-97.

A383 "Mechanism or design? A misleading dilemma." *University of Toronto Quarterly* 23/1 OC1953 1-9.

A384 "Modernism and the Cambridge Platonists." *Royal Society of Canada, Transactions* Third series 47/sect.2 1953 61-8.

A385 *Modernism past and present*. With a foreword by the Rt. Rev. Lord Bishop of Ripon. London: John Murray, 1932. xxix, 369p.

A386 "The Montaigne quater-centenary." *University of Toronto Quarterly* 3/2 1934 208-27.

A387 "Morality and convention." *Hibbert Journal* 16 JA1918 251-62.

A388 "Mrs. Humphrey Ward and the theological novel." *Hibbert Journal* 18 JL1920 675-86.

A389 "The need for a modern casuistry." *International Journal of Ethics* 24/4 JL1914 375-401.

A390 "A neglected Canadian man of letters." *Dalhousie Review* 1/4 JA1922 407-17. On John Beattie Crozier.

A391 *Nietzsche and the ideals of modern Germany.* London: Edward Arnold, 1915. xiv, 235p.

A392 "The personality of Thomas Hobbes." *Hibbert Journal* 47/2 JA1949 123-31.

A393 "A philosopher in politics (on Lord Balfour)." *Dalhousie Review* 10/2 1931 244-57.

A394 "A philosopher looks at the creeds." *Expository Times* 46 1934 260-4.

A395 "Philosophy in a world crisis." *University of Toronto Quarterly* 5/1 OC1935 105-17.

A396 "Philosophy in Renaissance art." *University of Toronto Quarterly* 10/4 JL1941 401-16.

A397 "The place of Coleridge in English theology." *Harvard Theological Review* 11/1 JA1918 1-31.

A398 "The Platonic Academy of Florence." *Hibbert Journal* 43 AL1945 226-36.

A399 "Power politics." *Queen's Quarterly* 53/2 1946 162-72.

A400 "The prophetic office of Mr. H.G. Wells." *International Journal of Ethics* 30/2 JA1920 172-89.

A401 "The puritanism of George Bernard Shaw." *Royal Society of Canada, Transactions* Third series 24/sect.2 1930 89-100.

A402 *Questions of the day in philosophy and psychology.* London: Edward Arnold, 1912. ix, 284p.

A403 "Rabelais, the humanist." *Personalist* 24 Autumn 1943 402-14.

A404 "Ralph Cudworth, the 'Latitude Man'." *Personalist* 32 Spring 1951 163-71.

A405 "Religion and world economy." *Dalhousie Review* 33 Summer 1953 81-7.

A406   "Religion in the Athens of Socrates." *University Magazine* 14/4 DC1915 491-505.

A407 "Religion in Soviet Russia." *Dalhousie Review* 27 AL1947 45-52.

A408   "Religious consciousness as a psychological fact." *Constructive Quarterly* 4 SE1916 467-81.

A409   "Religious difficulties in science." *University of Toronto Quarterly* 19/2 JN1950 165-9.

A410   "The 'reverent agnosticism' of Karl Barth." *Harvard Theological Review* 43/3 JL1950 215-32.

A411   "Schleiermacher, Ritschl, Barth: a sequence." *Hibbert Journal* 50 OC1951 10-7.

A412   "Scholastic philosophy in Renaissance thought." *Personalist* 27 Summer 1946 285-98.

A413   "Self-realization as the moral end." *International Journal of Ethics* 17 JL1907 483-9.

A414 "Sincerity, not policy, the first need of the churches." *Hibbert Journal* 16 JL1918 570-80.

A415   "Some ambiguities in 'democracy'." *American Journal of Sociology* 26/5 MR1920 545-57.

A416 "Spirit of Renaissance scientists." *Personalist* 22/3 JL1941 285-96.

A417   "The superseding of democracy." *Dalhousie Review* 30/2 JL1950 145-58.

A418   "The talents and foibles of Ernest Renan." *Dalhousie Review* 3 1923 362-75.

A419   "Theology and romanticism." *Harvard Theological Review* 13 OC1920 362-89.

A420 "Theories of the comic." *University Magazine* 19/1 1920 55-71.

A421 "Through modernism to humanism?" *Hibbert Journal* 52 AL1954 224-30.

A422 "Tolstoy as a problem in psycho-analysis." *Royal Society of Canada, Transactions* Third series 17/sect.2 1923 29-39.

A423 "Tragic drama: Aristotle's theory tested by Shakespeare's practice." *University Magazine* 16 OC1917 431-50.

A424 "The unexpurgated *Mein Kampf.*" *University of Toronto Quarterly* 8/4 JL1939 385-93.

A425 "Was Plato an ascetic?" *Philosophical Review* 24/6 NO1915 603-13.

A426 "What can one justly 'own'?" *Dalhousie Review* 31/1 AL1951 1-10.

A427 "Why the Reformation must be neither compromised nor explained away." *Hibbert Journal* 49 OC1950 32-40.

A428 "Wilfred Ward." *Hibbert Journal* 18 OC1919 61-93.

A429 "Wilfred Ward's reconciling attitude." *Constructive Quarterly* 8 JN1920 182-92.

TenBroeke, James 1859-1937

A430 *A constructive basis for theology.* London: Macmillan, 1914. ix, 400p. "Notes and references," p.379-95.

A431 *The moral life and religion; a study of moral and religious personality.* New York: Macmillan, 1922. 244p. "Notes and references," p.231-41.

A432 *A syllabus of lectures based on the metaphysics of Herman Lotze.* Toronto: Standard Publishing Co., 1898.

Tracy, Frederick 1862-1951

A433 "The autobiography of a philosophy." *American Journal of Theology* 8/4 OC1904 784-90. On Herbert Spencer's autobiography.

A434 "Bibliography of the language of childhood." *American Journal of Psychology* 6 1893 134-8.

A435 *Broken lights.* Toronto: University of Toronto Press, 1935. 140p. Essays on ethics, religious education and moral education.

A436 "Common ground (in philosophy and religion)." *Canadian Journal of Religious Thought* 4/5 SE-OC1927 393-400.

A437 "Conceptualism." *Hastings' Encyclopaedia of religion and ethics* Volume III. Edinburgh: T. & T. Clark, & New York: Scribner's, 1910. 799-800.

A438 "Experiment in religious education." *Religious Education* 9 AU1914 389-91.

A439   "Habit in the religious life." *Religious Education* 3 AL1908 10-3.

A440   "Immortality and the moral argument." *Crozer Quarterly* 12 AL1935 142-51.

A441   *Introductory educational psychology, a book for teachers in training.* By Frederick Tracy and Samuel Bower Sinclair. Toronto: Macmillan of Canada, 1909. 192p.

A442   *Jido Shinri-gaku.* Japanese tr. by Kojiro Matsumoto & Heisaburo Takashima of *Psychology of childhood.* Tokyo: Fukyusha, 1899. 312 + 10p.

A443   "Man's place in the universe." *Canadian Baptist* 20OC1904.

A444   "Materials of religious education in the family." *Religious Education* 11 AL1916 168-72.

A445   "The meaning of religious education." *Religious Education* 17 FE1922 3-8.

A446   "Plato, the modernist." *Canadian Journal of Religious Thought* 9/4 SE-OC1931 277-84.

A447   *Psychologie der Kindheit: eine Gesamtdarstellung der Kinderpsychologie für Seminaristen, Studierende und Lehrer.* Uebersetzung von Joseph Stimpfl. Leipzig: Wunderlich, 1899. xii, 150p. Tr. of *Psychology of childhood.*

A448   *Psychologie der Kindheit: eine Gesamtdarstellung der Kinderpsychologie für Seminaristen, Studierende and Lehrer.* 2 Aufl. Von Frederick Tracy & Joseph Stimpfl. Uebersetzt von Joseph Stimpfl. Leipzig: Wunderlich, 1908. vii, 178p. New ed. of A447, enlarged by Stimpfl.

A449   *Psychologie der Kindheit...3 Aufl.* Von Frederick Tracy & Joseph Stimpfl. Leipzig: E. Wunderlich, 1909. vii, 181p.

A450   *Psychologie der Kindheit...4 Aufl.* Von Frederick Tracy & Joseph Stimpfl. Leipzig: E. Wunderlich, 1912. vii, 198p.

A451   *The psychology of adolescence.* New York: Macmillan, 1920. x, 246p. Bibliography, p.236-43. Repr. 1921, 1922, 1923, 1926, 1927, 1930, 1938. (Handbooks of Moral and Religious Education, no.2. Ed. by E.H. Sneath.)

A452   *The psychology of childhood.* Boston: Heath, 1893. 94p. Bibliography, p.91-4. Published version of author's Ph.D. dissertation, Clark University.

A453 *The psychology of childhood.* 2ed. Boston: D.C. Heath & Co., 1894. xiii, 170p. Bibliography, p.161-7. (Heath's Pedagogical Library). Repr. "3ed.," 1896; "4ed.," 1897.

A454 *The psychology of childhood.* 5ed. rev. & enlarged by the addition of a new chapter on the "Aesthetic, moral and religious aspects of mind development." Boston: D.C. Heath, 1901. x, 176p. Repr. "6ed.," 1896.

A455 *The psychology of childhood.* By Frederick Tracy and Joseph Stimpfl. 7ed. rev. and enlarged by material from the German edition. Boston: D.C. Heath & Co., 1909. x, 219p. (Heath's Pedagogical Library).

A456 "A scientific basis for religious and moral education from the standpoint of ethics." *Religious Education Association, Proceedings* 1904.

A457 "The Scottish philosophy." *University of Toronto Quarterly* 2/1 NO1895 1-15.

A458 "The Socratic method." *Ontario Normal College Monthly* NO&DC1906 & FE1907.

A459 *A syllabus of logic; with questions and exercises for the use of students.* Toronto: University of Toronto, 1903. 32p. Bibliography, p3.

A460 *The teacher and the school; studies in teaching and organization.* Toronto: R.D. Fraser, 1909. 64p.

A461 "Testimony from science and philosophy concerning the future of life." *American Journal of Theology* 10/1 JA1906 169-71. On books by Münsterberg & Hyslop.

A462 "Theories of knowledge in relation to teaching." *Ontario Education Association, Proceedings* 1902.

A463 "Total depravity." *Canadian Journal of Religious Thought* 6/4 JL-AU1929 249-58.

A464 "What is human nature?" *Religious Education* 18 FE1923 10-3.

A465 Review of James Mark Baldwin, *Mental development in the child and the race. Philosophical Review* 4/4 JL1895 423-7.

Watson, John 1847-1939

A466 "The absolute and the time-process." *Philosophical Review* 4 1895 353-70, 486-505.

A467 "Aristotle's posterior analytics." *Philosophical Review* 13 1904 1-15, 143-58.

A468 "Art, morality and religion." *Queen's Quarterly* 5 1898 287-96 & 6 1898 132-53.

A469 Article on the nature of a university. *Queen's Journal* 30OC1888 183.

A470 "Balfour's 'Foundations of belief'." *Queen's Quarterly* 3 1896 241-61 & 4 1896-7 14-29, 93-104, 181-88.

A471 "Bosanquet on mind and the Absolute." *Philosophical Review* 34 1925 427-42.

A472 "Browning's interpretation of the 'Alcestis'." *Queen's Quarterly* 3 1895 41-9, 93-106.

A473 "The Cartesian *cogito ergo sum* and Kant's criticism of rational psychology." *Kantstudien* 2/1 1898 22-49.

A474 "Christianity and history." *Queen's Quarterly* 15 1908 163-75.

A475 *Christianity and idealism; the Christian ideal of life in its relation to the Greek and Jewish ideals and to modern philosophy.* New York: Macmillan, 1896. Originally a series of lectures given before the Philosophical Union of the University of California. (Publications of the Philosophical Union of the University of California, 2).

A476 *Christianity and idealism, the Christian ideal of life in its relation to the Greek and Jewish ideals and to modern philosophy.* 2ed., with additions. New York & London: Macmillan, & Glasgow: J. Maclehose, 1897. xxxvi, 292p. Published version of a series of lectures given before the Philosophical Union of the University of California.

A477 "Christianity and modern life." *Sunday afternoon lectures in Convocation Hall, Queen's University, Kingston, Session 1890-91.* Kingston: Published by the students, 1891. 30-7.

A478 *Comte, Mill and Spencer; an outline of philosophy.* Glasgow: J. Maclehose & Sons, & New York: Macmillan, 1895. 302p. Later, expanded edition published as *An outline of philosophy.*

A479 "Conflict of absolutism and realism." *Philosophical Review* 33 1924 229-44.

A480 "The conflict of idealism and realism; a symposium held in Glasgow University in the year of Our Lord one thousand nine hundred and seven." *Queen's Quarterly* 31 1924 343-64 & 32 1924 14-42, 104-18.

A481 "The critical philosophy and idealism." *Philosophical Review* 1/1 JA1892 9-23. The first article, apart from an introductory editorial, to be published in the journal. Written on invitation by Jacob Gould Schurman. cf. A.B. McKillop, *A disciplined intelligence*, p.202.

A482   "The critical philosophy in its relations to realism and sensationalism." Read to the Concord School of Philosophy August 3, 1881. *Journal of Speculative Philosophy* 15 1881 337-60.

A483   "Dante and medieval thought." *Queen's Quarterly* 1 1894 253-66; 2 1894 25-38, 110-22; 2 1895 235-48, 269-87.

A484   "Dante and medieval thought: Chancellor Fleming's lectureship." *Queen's Quarterly* 1 1893 114-9.

A485   "Darwinism and morality." *Canadian Monthly and National Review* 10 OC1876 319-26.

A486   "The days of Principal Grant." *Queen's Journal* 51/32 17FE1925 3.

A487   "The degree of Ph.D. in philosophy." *Queen's Quarterly* 8 1900 73-5.

A488   "Democracy and the universities." *Queen's Quarterly* 33 1926 355-63.

A489   "A discussion of Dr. Whitehead's philosophy of nature with special reference to his work *Concept of nature.*" *Actes du 8e Congrès International de Philosophie à Prague, 2-7 sept. 1934.* Prague: Comité d'Organisation du Congrès, 1936. 903-9.

A490   *Education and life; an address delivered at the opening of the thirty-second session of Queen's University, Kingston.* Kingston: William Bailie for the Alma Mater Society of Queen's University, 1873. 27p.

A491   "Edward Caird." *Philosophical Review* 18 JA1909 108-10.

A492   "Edward Caird as teacher and thinker." *Queen's Quarterly* 16 AL-JN1909 303-13.

A493   "Empiricism and common logic." *Journal of Speculative Philosophy* 10 JA1876 17-36.

A494   "The ethical aspects of Darwinism; a rejoinder." *Canadian Monthly and National Review* 11/6 JN1877 638-44.

A495   "The form and content of the *Divina commedia.*" *Queen's Quarterly* 2 1895 235-48. Part 4 of "Dante and medieval thought." cf. A472.

A496   "Forty years of Queen's." *Queen's Journal* 39/24 31JA1913 3-4.

A497   "The future of our universities," an address. *Queen's Journal* 15/12 30OC1888 183-5.

A498   "G.W. Leibnitz and Protestant theology." *New World* 5 1896 102-22.

A499   "German philosophy and politics." *Queen's Quarterly* 22 1915 329-44.

A500   "German philosophy and the war." *Queen's Quarterly* 23 1916 365-79.

A501   "Gnostic theology." *Queen's Quarterly* 7 1900 259-84 & 8 1900 1-15.

A502   "The Greek mysteries." *Queen's Quarterly* 37 1930 633-47.

A503   "Hedonism and utilitarianism." *Journal of Speculative Philosophy* 10 1876 271-90.

A504   *Hedonistic theories from Aristippus to Spencer.* Glasgow: J. Maclehose & Sons, & New York: Macmillan, 1895. 248p.

A505   "Hell, purgatory and paradise." *Queen's Quarterly* 2 1895 269-87. Part 5 of "Dante and medieval thought." cf. A483.

A506   "The higher life of the scholar," university sermon. *Queen's Journal* 27/5 21DC1899 88-92.

A507   "Humanism," a lecture. *Queen's Journal* 32/7 1FE1905 283-91 & 32/8 16FE1905 313-9.

A508   "Humanism." *Queen's Quarterly* 13 1905 106-26.

A509   "The ideal life," an address. *Queen's Journal* 15/7 26FE1888 101-4.

A510   "The ideal life." *Sunday afternoon address in Convocation Hall, Queen's University, Kingston, Ontario, Session 1890-91.* Kingston: Published by the students, 1891. 23-9.

A511   "The idealism of Edward Caird." *Philosophical Review* 18 MR1909 147-63, 259-80.

A512   *The interpretation of religious experience; the Gifford Lectures delivered in the University of Glasgow in the years 1910-12.* Glasgow: J. Maclehose & Sons, 1912. 2 vols. Vol. 1, Historical; vol. 2, Constructive.

A513   *Kant and his English critics; a comparison of critical and empirical philosophy.* Kingston: Stacey & Walpole, Glasgow: J. Maclehose & Sons, & New York: Macmillan, 1881. 402p.

A514 "Kant on the infinite divisibility of space." *Journal of Speculative Philosophy* 20/2 AL1886 219-21. Excerpt from *Kant and his English critics.*

A515 "Kant's principles of judgement." *Journal of Speculative Philosophy* 14 OC1880 376-98.

A516 "Kant's reply to Hume." *Journal of Speculative Philosophy* 10 AL1876 113-34.

A517 "The later stages in Greek religion." *Queen's Quarterly* 35 1928 347-57.

A518 "Leslie Stephen's 'The utilitarians'," a critical notice. *Queen's Quarterly* 9 1901 57-60.

A519 "Lessing as art-critic." *Queen's Quarterly* 15 1907 54-61.

A520 "The makers of Queen's; James Williamson, L.L.D." *Queen's Review* 1/3 MA1927 67-9.

A521 "Metaphysics and psychology." *Philosophical Review* 2 1893 513-28.

A522 "The metaphysics of Aristotle." *Philosophical Review* 7 1898 23-42, 113-34, 248-75, 337-54.

A523 "The method of Kant." *Mind* 5 1880 528-48.

A524 "The middle ages and the reformation." *Queen's Quarterly* 1 JL1893 4-11.

A525 "Mr. Rashdall's defence of personal idealism." *Mind* N.S.18 1909 244-51.

A526 "Mr. Spencer's derivation of space." *Mind* 15 OC1890 537-44.

A527 "The new 'ethical' philosophy." *International Journal of Ethics* 9 1899 413-34.

A528 "Nietzsche's *Genealogy of morals*." *Queen's Quarterly* 6 1898 35-55.

A529 *An outline of philosophy, with notes historical and critical.* 2ed., with additions, of *Comte, Mill and Spencer.* Glasgow: J. Maclehose & Sons, & New York: Macmillan, 1898. 489p. 3ed., 1901; 4ed., 1908.

A530 "The outlook in philosophy." *Queen's Quarterly* 8 1901 241-56.

A531 "A phase of modern thought," an address. *Queen's Journal* N.S.2/1 25OC1879 4-7.

A532   A phase of modern thought." *Rose-Belford's Canadian Monthly* 3 NO1879 457-72.

A533   "Philo and the New Testament." *Queen's Quarterly* 7 1899 33-50, 81-100.

A534   *Philo and the New Testament, synopsis of lectures with extracts from Philo*...Kingston: Bailie, 1899. 27p. (Theological Alumni Conference of Queen's University).

A535   *The philosophical basis of religion; a series of lectures.* Glasgow: J. Maclehose & Sons, 1907. 485p. Based on presentations before the Brooklyn Institute of Arts and Sciences.

A536   *The philosophy of John Stuart Mill as contained in extracts from his own writings.* Selected by John Watson. Kingston: William Bailie, 1891. Repr. Kingston: Jackson Press, 1908.

A537   *The philosophy of Kant as contained in extracts from his own writings.* Selected and translated by John Watson. Glasgow: James Maclehose & Sons, 1888. 2ed., 1891, Repr. 1894, 1897. New ed., 1901, Repr. 1908. 3ed., 1919. A revision of an 1882 collection, cf. no. A540.

A538   *The philosophy of Kant as contained in extracts from his own writings.* Selected and translated by John Watson. New ed. Glasgow: Maclehose, 1923. x, 356p. Repr. Glasgow: Jackson Wylie, 1927.

A539   *The philosophy of Kant explained.* Glasgow: J. Maclehose & Sons, 1908. 515p.

A540   *The philosophy of Kant in extracts.* Selected by John Watson. Kingston: William Bailie, 1882.

A541   "Philosophy of Plotinus." *Philosophical Review* 37 1928 482-500.

A542   "Plato and Protagoras." *Philosophical Review* 16 1907 469-87.

A543   "Plato's theory of education." *Presbyterian Review* 8 385- .

A544   "The politics of Dante." *Queen's Quarterly* 2 1894 110-22. Part 3 of "Dante and medieval thought," no. A471.

A545   "Pragmatism and idealism." *Queen's Quarterly* 21 1914 465-72.

A546   "Principal Grant's 'Religion (sic) of the world'." *Queen's Journal* 51/38 31MR1925 1,8.

A547   "The problem of Hegel." *Philosophical Review* 3 1894 546-67.

A548   "Professor Tyndall's 'Materialism'." *Rose-Belford's Canadian Monthly* 1 MR1878 282-8.

A549 "Recent theology and philosophy." *Queen's Quarterly* 7 1900 228-35. A review discussion of *Fundamental ideas of Christianity* by John Caird and *The Theaetetus of Plato* tr. with intro. by S.W. Dyde.

A550 "The relation of philosophy to ancient and modern cosmogonies." *Queen's Quarterly* 14 1906 134-48.

A551 *The relation of philosophy to science; an inaugural lecture delivered in the Convocation Hall of Queen's University, Kingston, Canada, on October 16th, 1872.* Kingston: William Bailie, 1872. 37p.

A552 "The relativity of knowledge. An examination of the doctrine as held by Mr. Herbert Spencer." *Journal of Speculative Philosophy* 11 JA1877 19-48.

A553 "Religion in the early Roman Empire." *Queen's Quarterly* 17 1910 333-41. Discussion of T.R. Glover, *The conflict of religions in the early Roman Empire.*

A554 "The religion of Greece." *Queen's Quarterly* 35 1928 219-28.

A555 "Reminiscences of college life." *Queen's Journal* 51/27 30JA1925 1.

A556 "Reminiscences of Dr. John Stewart." *Queen's Review* 3/5 MA1929 151-3.

A557 "Reminiscences of early days at Queen's University." *Queen's Journal* 51/36 6MR1925 3-5.

A558 Reply at the unveiling of his portrait, Queen's Theological College. *Queen's Journal* 28/2 9NO1900 42-6.

A559   "The sadness and joy of knowledge." *Queen's Journal* 28/10 15MR1901 231-3; 28/11 29MR1901 257-60.

A560 *Schelling's transcendental idealism; a critical exposition.* Chicago: Griggs, & London: Trübner, 1882. 251p. (German Philosophical Classics for English Readers and Students, ed. George S. Morris).

A561 "Science and religion, a reply to Prof. Tyndall on 'Materialism and its opponents'." *Canadian Monthly and National Review* 9/5 MA1876 384-97.

A562 "Sketches in evolution." *Knowledge* 12 241- .

A563   "Some remarks on Biblical criticism." *Queen's Journal* 22/2 7NO1894 23-7.

A564   "Some remarks on radical empiricism." *Queen's Quarterly* 18 1910 111-9.

A565   *The state in peace and war.* Glasgow: J. Maclehose & Sons, & Toronto: Macmillan, 1919. 296p.

A566   "The study and profession of medicine," a speech. *Queen's Journal* 12/4 13JA1885 46-7.

A567   "Symposium on the university question," Dr. Watson's remarks. *Queen's Quarterly* 8 1901 257-9. The comments of other symposiasts appear p.260-8.

A568   "The theology of Dante." *Queen's Quarterly* 1 1894 253-66. Part 1 of "Dante and medieval thought," no. A483.

A569   "The theology of Dante, part 2." *Queen's Quarterly* 2 1895 25-38. Part 2 of "Dante and medieval thought," no. A483.

A570   "Thirty years in the history of Queen's University." *Queen's Quarterly* 10 1902 188-96.

A571   "Thomas Aquinas." *Queen's Quarterly* 9 1902 264-76, 10 1902 58-71.

A572   "A typical New England philosopher." *Queen's Quarterly* 25 1918 282-91. On George Sylvester Morris.

A573   "The unity of science," an address. *Queen's Journal* 31/6 1FE1904 7-14.

A574   "The university and the schools." *Queen's Quarterly* 8 1901 323-40.

A575   "The university and the state," an address. *Queen's Journal* 26NO1898 23-8.

A576   "Utilitarian ethics." *The Week* 2/20 16AL1885. A discussion of F.R. Beattie's *An examination of the utilitarian theory of morals*, no. A3.

A577   "Wenley's *Kant and the philosophical revolution*." *Queen's Quarterly* 18 1911 303-8.

A578   "Wenley's *Stoicism and its influence*." *Anglican Theological Review* 8/4 AL1926 315-30. Critical discussion of a work by R.M. Wenley.

A579   "Winckelman and Greek art," prefatory to extracts from Winckelman translated by John McGillivray. *Queen's Quarterly* 1 1893 129.

A580 "The world as force, with special reference to the philosophy of Mr. Herbert Spencer." *Journal of Speculative Philosophy* 12 AL1878 113-37.

A581 "The world as force, with special reference to the philosophy of Mr. Herbert Spencer. II. The indestructibility of matter." *Journal of Speculative Philosophy* 13 AL1879 151-79.

A582 Review of Bernard Bosanquet, *The philosophical theory of the state*. *Queen's Quarterly* 7 1900 320-2.

A583 Review of Edward Caird, *Essays on literature*. *Queen's Quarterly* 16 1909 369.

A584 Review of John Caird, *University Sermons*. *Queen's Quarterly* 7 1899 153-4.

A585 Review of Georges Noël, *La Logique de Hegel*. *Philosophical Review* 6 1897 411-5.

A586 Review of Jacob Gould Schurman, *Agnosticism and religion*. *Philosophical Review* 5 1896 555-6. cf. A325.

A587 Review of Jacob Gould Schurman, *Kantian ethics and the ethics of evolution*. *Journal of Speculative Philosophy* 17 1883 101-4. cf. no. A330.

Willson, David 1778(?)-1866

A588 *The impressions of the mind: to which are added some remarks on church and state discipline and the acting principles of life.* Toronto: J.H. Lawrence, 1835. 358p.

Wright, Henry Wilkes 1878-1959

A589 "The basis of human association." *Journal of Philosophy* 17 1920 421-30.

A590 "Community as the key to evolution." *Journal of Philosophy* 28 1931 98-102.

A591 "The concept of psychological environment applied to the process of 'sublimation'." *Bulletin of the Canadian Psychological Association* 3 1943 50-2.

A592 "Culture and the modern world." *Quarterly Journal of the University of North Dakota* 12/3 AL1922.

A593 "Does the objective system of values imply a cosmic intelligence?" *International Journal of Ethics* 38 1928 284-94.

A594   "Dualism in psychology." *American Journal of Psychology* 53 1940 121-8.

A595   "Empirical idealism in outline." *Monist* 39 1929 45-57.

A596   "Ethics and mental hygiene." *International Journal of Ethics* 47 OC1936 25-44.

A597   "Ethics and social philosophy." *Monist* 36 OC1926 627-44. Repr. *Philosophy today: essays on recent developments in the field of philosophy.* Ed. Edward Leroy Schaub. Chicago: Open Court, 1928. 87-104. Repr. Freeport, N.Y.: Books for Libraries, 1968.

A598   "Evolution and ethical method." *International Journal of Ethics* 16 1905 59-68.

A599   "Evolution and the self-realization theory." *International Journal of Ethics* 18 1908 355-62.

A600   "Facing reality." *Journal of Abnormal and Social Psychology* 32 JL-SE1937 223-35.

A601   *Faith justified by progress; lectures delivered before Lake Forest College on the Foundation of the late William Bross.* New York: C. Scribner's Sons, 1916 (The Bross Library, ix).

A602   "The field concept in psychology." *Canadian Journal of Psychology* 1 1947 41-3.

A603   *Idealism and social progress, being an inaugural lecture.* Winnipeg: University of Manitoba, 1921.

A604   "Intellect and the development of personality." *American Journal of Psychology* 57 1944 371-88.

A605   "The intellect vs. emotion in political cooperation." *Ethics* 56 OC1945 19-29.

A606   "Intellectual freedom and political cooperation." *University of Toronto Quarterly* 14/3 1945 240-9.

A607   "Is the dualism of mind and matter final?" *Philosophical essays in honour of James Edwin Creighton.* New York: Macmillan, 1917. 184-201.

A608   "Mechanism and mind in present-day social life." *Manitoba Essays.* Ed. Rupert Clendon Lodge. Toronto: Macmillan, 1937. 372-402. cf. A186.

A609   "The metaphysical implications of human association." *Philosophical Review* 38/1 JA1929 54-68.

A610   *The moral standard of democracy.* New York & London: D. Appleton & Co., 1925. ix, 309p.

A611   "Natural selection in childhood." *Philosophical Review* 14 1905 40-56.

A612   "The nature and function of context in communication." *Canadian Journal of Psychology* 2 1948 49-52.

A613   "Note on communication as a principle of metaphysical synthesis." *Journal of Philosophy* 56 1959 730-3.

A614   "The object of perception versus the object of thought." *Journal of Philosophy* 13 1916 437-41.

A615   "Objective values." *International Journal of Ethics* 42 AL1932 255-72.

A616   "Objectivity of moral values." *Philosophical Review* 32 JL1923 385-400.

A617   "Pitfalls in personal development." *The Canadian Credit Institute Bulletin* 62 MA1936 1- .

A618   "A plea for eclecticism." *Philosophical essays presented to John Watson.* Kingston: Queen's University, 1922. 254-74.

A619   "Practical success as the criterion of truth." *Philosophical Review* 22 NO1913 606-22.

A620   "Principles of voluntarism." *Philosophical Review* 24 1915 297-313.

A621   "The problem of altruistic motivation." *Bulletin of the Canadian Psychological Association* 6 1946 82-3.

A622   "Problem of altruistic motivation in the light of modern psychology." *University of Toronto Quarterly* 16 JA1947 157-68.

A623   "The problem of the criminal in the light of some modern conceptions." *Journal of the American Medical Association* 61 1913 2119-22.

A624   "The psychological centrality of communication." *Canadian Journal of Psychology* 1 1947 92-5.

A625   "A psychological study of the nature of mental deficiency." *Psychological Bulletin* 37 1940 572.

A626   "Psychological worlds." *Journal of Philosophy* 38/23 23OC1941 600-8.

A627   "The psychologist's world." *Bulletin of the Canadian Psychological Association* 28AL1941.

A628   "Psychology in Canada." *Culture* SE1940 327-32.

A629   "The psychology of social culture." *American Journal of Psychology* 52 1939 210-26.

A630   "Rational self-interest and the social adjustment." *International Journal of Ethics* 30 1920 394-422.

A631   "Religion and morality." *International Journal of Ethics* 20 1909 87-93.

A632   *The religious response; an introduction to the philosophy of religion.* New York: Harper and Bros., 1929. 256p.

A633   "The role of the intellect in democratic morals." *Bulletin of the Canadian Psychological Association* 4 1944 64-5.

A634   *Self-realization: an outline of ethics.* New York: Harper & Brothers, 1913. 429p.

A635   "Self-realization and the criterion of goodness." *Philosophical Review* 17 1908 606-18.

A636   "The significance of communication for psychological theory." *Canadian Journal of Psychology* 8 1954 32-40.

A637   "Social significance." *American Journal of Psychology* 49 JA1937 49-57.

A638   "The social significance of education." *Philosophical Review* 28 1919 345-69.

A639   "Some modern phases of psychology." *Medical Record* 1917 584-7.

A640   "Spirit and matter: a reply to Dr. Dashiell." *Journal of Philosophy* 14 1917 400-3.

A641   "The thirteenth annual meeting of the Western Philosophical Association." *Journal of Philosophy* 10 1913 319-26.

A642   "The three contexts of human behaviour." *Psychological Review* 50 1943 351-69.

A643   "Three kinds of agreement." *University of Toronto Quarterly* 6/1 OC1936 66-88.

A644   "Three theories of the psychology of meaning." *Canadian Journal of Psychology* 3 1949 80-8.

A645 "The truth in ascetic theories of morality." *Philosophical Review* 10/6 NO1901 601-18.

A646 "The twelfth annual meeting of the Western Philosophical Association." *Journal of Philosophy* 9 1912 350-7.

A647 "The two aspects of meaning." *Canadian Journal of Psychology* 4 1950 156-70.

A648 "Understanding human conduct and social relations." *University of Toronto Quarterly* 3 1934 321-48.

A649 "Value, subjective and objective." *Journal of Philosophy* 23 1926 378-86.

A650 "The values of democracy." *University of Toronto Quarterly* 10/1 OC1940 68-88.

A651 " The values of personal association." *Ethics* 52/4 JL1942 447-62.

A652 "What alternatives can religion present to the will of modern man?" *Journal of Religion* 1 JL1921 407-15.

Young, George Paxton 1818-1889

A653 *The ethics of freedom.* Ed. by James Gibson Hume. Toronto: University of Toronto Press, 1911. 76p. Includes a repr. of A656 together with a note on Young and notes from Young's lectures, both by Hume.

A654 "An examination of Legendre's proof of the properties of parallel lines." *The Canadian Journal of Industry, Science, and Art* N.S.1/6 NO1856 519-22.

A655 "An examination of Professor Ferrier's theory of knowing and being." *The Canadian Journal of Industry, Science and Art* N.S.1/2 FE1856 105-26.

A656 *Freedom and necessity: a lecture.* Toronto: Adam, Stevenson & Co., 1870. 19p. Repr. in A653.

A657 "Lecture delivered at Knox College, May 1855." *The Toronto Globe* 15MA1855. 1p. On Sir William Hamilton's doctrine of sensitive perception.

A658 "Lecture on the philosophical principles of natural religion." *The Home and Foreign Record of the Canada Presbyterian Church* 2/2 DC1862 29-38.

A659   *Miscellaneous discourses and expositions of scripture.* Edinburgh: Johnstone, 1854. vii, 348p.

A660   "A new proof of the parallelogram of forces." *The Canadian Journal of Industry, Science and Art* N.S.1/4 JL1856 357-9.

A661   "Notes on passages in the Platonic dialogues." *The Canadian Journal of Industry, Science and Art* N.S.7/42 NO1862 477-83.

A662   "On Sir David Brewster's supposed law of visible direction." *The Canadian Journal of Industry, Science and Art* N.S.2/10 JL1857 268-76.

A663   "Resolution of algebraical equations." *The Canadian Journal of Industry, Science and Art* N.S.5/25 JA1860 20-41. "Proof of the impossibility of representing in finite algebraical functions, in the most general case, the roots of algebraical equations of degrees higher than the fourth..."

A664   "Relation of the law of gravitation to the principle of the conservation of energy; with a proof of the necessary transformation of the force of gravity, at a certain limit, from a force of attraction to one of repulsion." *The Canadian Journal of Industry, Science and Art* N.S.14/88 DC1875 589-96.

A665   "The relation which can be proved to subsist between the area of a plane triangle and the sum of the angles, on the hypothesis that Euclid's 12th axiom is false." *The Canadian Journal of Industry, Science and Art* N.S.5/28 JL1860 341-58.

A666   "Remarks on Professor Boole's Mathematical theory of the laws of thought." *The Canadian Journal of Industry, Science and Art* N.S.10/57 MA1865 161-82.

A667   Review of Alexander C. Fraser, *Rational philosophy in history and in system. The Canadian Journal of Industry, Science and Art* N.S.3/16 JL1858 347-56.

A668   Review of Sir William Hamilton, *The philosophy of Sir William Hamilton, Bart.* Ed. by O.W. Wright. *The Canadian Journal of Industry, Science and Art.* N.S.1/4 JL1856 379-86. At top of p380-5: "Reviews--the validity of consciousness."

A669   Review of James McCosh, *Typical forms and special ends in creation.* By James McCosh and George Dickie. *The Canadian Journal of Industry, Science and Art* N.S.1/6 NO1856 528-41.

A670   Review of Thomas Reid, *Reid's works (Essays on the human mind, etc.) with selections from his unpublished letters; with a preface note and supplementary dissertation by Sir William Hamilton, Bart. The Canadian*

Journal of Industry, Science and Art N.S.2/10 JL1857 285-99. On Hamilton as well as on Reid.

Index of research tools mentioned in the text

Index des instruments de recherche renseignés dans la texte

Canadian Periodicals Which Contain Articles of Philosophical Relevance

Périodiques canadiens qui contiennent articles d'interêt philosophique

** designates a primarily philosophical journal/indique une revue savante essentiellement philosophique.

* designates a scholarly review with frequent philosophical contributions/indique une revue savante publiante souvent des contributions philosophiques.

*** designates a scholarly review with occasional philosophical contributions/ indique une revue savante publiante parfois des contributions philosophiques.

! designates a philosophical review containing much student writing/indique une revue philosophique publiante des écrits d'étudiants.

L'Academie Canadienne St. Thomas d'Aquin. Québec. 1930-45.

Acta Victoriana. Cobourg, Toronto. 1878-1932.

L'Action Canadienne-français. Montréal. 1917-28.

L'Action Nationale. Montréal. 1933- .

L'Action Universitaire. Montréal. 1934-54.

Amérique Française. Montréal. 1941-55, 63- .

L'Ami du Peuple de l'ordre et des Lois. Montréal. 1832-40.

Annales de l'ACFAS. Montréal. 1935- .   ***

Basilian. Toronto. 1935-7.

Basilian Teacher. Toronto. 1956- .

Biology and Philosophy. Guelph. 1986 - .

Brèches. Montréal. 1972- .

Bulletin de la Cercle Gabriel Marcel. Montreal 1978. **

Bulletin de la Société de Philosophie du Québec. Montréal.   1974. **

Cahiers de Cap-Rouge. Cap-Rouge. 1972- .

Le Canada Français. Québec. 1888-91.

Le Canada Français. Québec. 1918-46.

Canadian Forum. Toronto. 1920- .

Canadian Journal. Toronto. 1852-78.

Canadian Journal of Economics and Political Science. Toronto. 1935-67. ***

Canadian Journal of Philosophy. Lethbridge. 1971- **

Canadian Journal of Political Science. Toronto. 1968- ***

Canadian Journal of Psychology. Toronto. 1947- ***

Canadian Journal of Political and Social Theory. Winnipeg. 1977- *

Canadian Journal of Religious Thought. Toronto. 1924-32. ***

Canadian Journal of Theology. Toronto. 1955-70. ***

Canadian Magazine. Toronto. 1893-1939.

Canadian Monthly and National Review. Toronto. 1872-82.

Canadian Philosophical Reviews/Revue Canadienne des Comptes Rendus en Philosophie. Edmonton. 1981- **

The Canadian Psychologist. Ottawa. 1950- *** .

Carleton University Student Journal of Philosophy. Ottawa. 1974- !

Carrefour. Ottawa. 1979- .

The Christian Guardian. Toronto. 1829-1925.

Cirpho. Montréal. 1973- **

Cité Libre. Montréal. 1957-66.

Collège et Famille. Montréal. 1944- (devint Education et Société).

Communications. Québec. 1978- ***

Contributions à l'Etude des Sciences de l'Homme. Montréal. 1952- .

Courrier du Canada. Québec. 1857-73.

Critère. Montréal. 1970- **

Culture. Québec. 1940-70. ***

Dalhousie Review. Halifax. 1921- ***

De Philosophia. Ottawa. 1980- !

Dialogue. Waterloo, Montréal. 1962- **

Dionysius. Halifax. 1977. *

Echo du Cabinet de Lecture Paroissal de Montréal. Montréal. 1859-73.

Echo des Pays, Industrie, Propriété et Union. St.-Charles. 1833-6.

Ecole Sociale Populaire. Montréal. 1911-49.

Eglise et Théologie. Ottawa. 1970- ***

Emergences. Montréal. 1966-7. !

Enseignement Secondaire au Canada. Québec. 1915-67.

Erasmus in English. Toronto. 1970-   ***

Esquisses: Philosophie et Littérature. Sorel. 1984- *

Ethics in Education. Toronto. 1981- **

Explorations. Toronto. 1953-9.

Fragments: Philosophie Québécoise; Philosophie au Québec. Trois-Rivières. 1982- **

Gants du Ciel. Montréal. 1953-6.

Gnosis. Montréal (Concordia). 1973- **

Historia Mathematica. Toronto. 1974- ***

Humanist in Canada. Victoria. 1967- **

Hume Studies. London, Ont. 1975- **

Informal Logic. Windsor. 1978- **

Information Médicale et Paramédicale. Montréal. 1949- .

International Journal. Toronto. 1946- .

Journal of Agricultural Ethics. Guelph. 1987- **

Journal of Business Ethics. Guelph. 1981- **

Journal of Indian Philosophy. Toronto. 1970- . Transferred to Oxford, U.K. **

Journal of Philosophical Logic. Toronto. 1971 Transferred to Pittsburgh, PA. **

Journal of the Philosophy of Sport. London. 1974- **

Journées Thomistes. Ottawa. 1935-6. *

Laurentian University Review. Sudbury. 1968- ***

Laval Théologique et Philosophique. Québec. 1945- *

Liberté. Montréal. 1959- .

Maintenant (Dominicains). Montréal. 1962- .

Manitoba Arts Review. Winnipeg. 1938-65. ***

Mediaeval Studies. Toronto. 1939- *

Mill Newsletter. Toronto. 1965- **

Mosaic. Winnipeg. 1968- ***

Nos Cahiers. Québec. 1936-39.

La Nouvelle France. Québec. 1902-18.

Ordre Nouveau. Montréal. 1936-40.

Parti Pris. Montréal. 1963-68.

La Petite Revue de Philosophie. Longueuil. 1979- **

Phi Zéro. Montréal. 1971- !

Philosopher. Ecrire et Lire. Montréal. 1985- **

Philosophie au Collège. Montréal. 1984- **

Philosophiques. Sherbrooke. 1974- **

Philosophy of Science. London, Ontario. 1934- ** Transferred from U.S.

Philosophy of the Social Sciences. Downsview. 1971- **

Phoenix. Toronto. 1946- *

Protée. Chicoutimi. 1970- .

Quartier Latin. Montréal. 1919- !

Queen's Quarterly. Kingston. 1893- ***

Recherches Sémiotiques /Semiotic Inquiry. Toronto. 1980- was the Canadian Journal of Research in Semiotics/Journal Canadien de Recherche Semiotigue. 1973-80. ***

Relations. Montréal. 1941- .

La Relève. Montréal. 1934-41, aussi La Nouvelle Relève. Montréal. 1941-8.

Renaissance and Reformation/Renaissance et Réforme. Toronto. 1964-. ***

Revue Canadienne. Montréal. 1864-1922.

Revue Canadienne: Journal Scientifique et Littéraire. Montréal. 1845-8.

Revue de l'Université de Moncton Moncton. 1968- ***

Revue de l'Université d'Ottawa. Ottawa. 1931- *

Revue de l'Université Laval. Québec. 1946- **

Revue et Corrigée. Montréal. 1981- .

Revue Trimestrielle Canadienne. Montréal. 1915 -. (devint L'Ingenieur. 1954).

Le Rosaire. Saint-Hyacinthe. 1895-1915. (devint Revue Dominicaine. 1915-62).

Russell: Journal of the Bertrand Russell Archives. Hamilton. 1971- **

Science et Esprit. Montréal. 1968- *

Sciences Ecclésiastiques. Montréal. 1948-67. *

Secular Thought. Toronto. 1885-1911.

Social Indicators Research. Guelph 1969 - ***

Social Praxis. Toronto. 1973- **

Stratégie. Longueuil. 1972- .

Studies in Religion/Sciences Religieuses. Toronto. 1971- ***

Ultimate Reality and Meaning. Toronto (Regis College). 1978- . **

The University Magazine. Montréal. 1901-20. ***

University of Toronto Monthly. Toronto. 1900- .

University of Toronto Quarterly. Toronto. 1895-6. ***

University of Toronto Quarterly. Toronto. 1931- ***

Le Vol du Hibou. Trois-Rivières. 1982- *

The Week. Toronto. 1883-96.

Westminster Institute Review. London. 1981-4. **

Subject Index/Index des sujets

The numbers in the index refer to entry numbers in Part II/Les numéros dans l'index ramènent aux numéros des notices en la deuxième partie.